LOCK KEEPER'S D

This Edition published 1996 by
Brewin Books,
Doric House,
56 Alcester Road,
Studley,
Warwickshire, B80 7LG

First Edition published by Shepperton Swan Ltd 1986

ISBN 1 85858 075 7

Typeset in Century Book by Avon Dataset Ltd, Bidford on Avon, Warks, B50 4JH
Printed by Heron Press, Kings Norton, Birmingham, B38 9TS

Lock Keeper's Daughter

A Worcestershire Canal Childhood

BY

Pat Warner

BREWIN BOOKS

To my family, for listening
and to the men of Tardebigge Canal . . .
wherever they may be.

Acknowledgements

For help received in writing this book, the Author would like to thank the Rev. D. Copley, Vicar of Tardebigge; Mr Chapman, Deputy Governor and his Staff at H.M.P. Hewell Grange; the residents of Hewell and Tardebigge, past and present; the Staff of Redditch Library; Midland Red Fares Office; Birmingham Cooperative Society; Mr S. Perry of the British Waterways Board; the men of the Worcester & Birmingham Canal; the family of the late George Bates B.E.M.; her family and friends for their patience and encouragement. And all those who kindly supplied illustrations. These are:

Eric de Maré: page vi; David Hill: pages 40 and 41; Cadbury-Schweppes Ltd: page 48; Frank Colledge: pages 68; Bromsgrove & Redditch Advertiser: page 93; Paul Smith: page 93; Peter Hill: page 61, 62, 65, 75, 76 and 85; Mrs H. Badger: page 96; Ruby Gwynne: page 99. All other illustrations are from the Author's Collection.

The Author

Mrs Pat Hill (née Warner) was born in a lock cottage on the Worcester & Birmingham Canal. She achieved a childhood ambition and was District Nurse in the Redditch and Bromsgrove area for twenty years. On the occasion of the Royal College of Nursing Diamond Jubilee in 1976, she was presented to H.M. the Queen at St James's Palace.

Since 1979, she has been Practice Nurse with a local Doctor. She has lived for many years with her family at Astwood Bank, near Redditch and has several grandchildren nearby.

Interests include Yoga, swimming and helping her husband with the smallholding around their house. Inhabitants of the property include a pony, donkey, goats, chickens and a dog.

Contents

Introduction			1
Chapter	1	The First Years	3
	2	The Special Days	28
	3	The Cut	54
	4	Christmas Memories	81
	5	Halfway House	86
	6	School Days	92
	7	My Heroine	105
	8	Hewell	111
	9	Life Around the Reservoir	119
	10	Epilogue	130
Maps		Tardebigge and surrounding area	36
		The Worcester & Birmingham Canal	137

Tardebigge lock keeper John Warner (1880–1952). Photographed at work in 1948 by Eric de Maré.

Introduction

TARDEBIGGE is a small parish, situated between Bromsgrove and Redditch, in the County of Worcestershire. Through its heart runs a section of the Worcester & Birmingham Canal with a series of thirty narrow beam locks – the longest flight in Britain. There is a wharf with dry dock, maintenance shops and a few houses I)\ Tardebigge Tunnel and along the towing path a few isolated cottages that were the lock keepers' houses. I was born in one and spent my childhood with the families who worked the narrow boats and the fishermen who came to the reservoir alongside.

We were very poor, even by the standards of the 1920s and 30s. Although my upbringing was in many ways a strange one, it was generally happy. So much has changed over the passing years that I felt I should record that vanished way of life, our association with the Earl of Plymouth's family on the Hewell Estate and my memories of the ordinary people who together made our village what it was.

It was my family that encouraged me to write this story as a record of days now gone: a way of life that will never be repeated.

PAT WARNER
The White House,
Astwood Hill,
Astwood Bank, Near Redditch,
Worcestershire.
1985.

Mother and Father at the back of the cottage, overlooking the Reservoir, July 1924, several months after I was born.

The First Years

Just a song and a swig
And a carefree half hour
Down at the old Halfway.
But there's always the love
Of a little girl,
Born on St. Patrick's day.

THROUGHOUT my early childhood I was referred to by my Father as "the scrapings of the pot" after arriving in a great hurry and shattering the peace of the Tardebigge countryside on March 17, 1924. 1 was a great surprise to my Mother who had been firmly convinced by the family doctor that "It" was a growth.

My Mother was then aged forty eight. She died a few months after my third birthday, so I do not remember her.

When I was born, our home was situated on the banks of the Tardebigge Reservoir, at the side of the Worcester & Birmingham Canal's Lock 53. My parents had lived there since 1909. Father was a Gloucestershire man, born in the Forest of Dean. He had a large number of brothers and sisters: by the time I knew them, Harry, the eldest, lived in Coventry; then came Uncle Sam, a sergeant at the police station in Ombersley, Worcestershire; Uncle Fred had lived on the Wharf at Tardebigge as a young married man; Father was next, followed by Uncle Will who was keeper at Tardebigge Top Lock. Uncle Dick, the youngest, lived in Wolverhampton and worked on the railway. During the First World War, there was a time when the canal at Tardebigge was virtually run by the Warner Brothers, Fred, John and Will. In addition there were two sisters, Aunt Edith and Aunt Mary, who both lived in Birmingham.

Father moved to Tardebigge with his parents and it was here that he met my Mother, then a children's nanny, in employment at King's Norton. Her name was Agnes Crumpton: John Warner's "Little Lassie", his most cherished possession. The Crumptons had also been canal workers in the 19th century.

Before setting up home in Tardebigge, they lived on the canal at Worcester in a building known as "The Blockhouse". Here they reared five daughters: Eva, Isobel, Kathleen, Phyllis and Margaret. At this time Father was employed as a labourer and Mother was taking in outwork from a clothing factory: this involved stitching the seams of mens' shirts on a sewing machine for which she was paid one farthing per shirt.

It was a great relief to Father when a lock keeper's job was offered to him back at Tardebigge. This meant a steady wage and a responsible position.

Not long after they had settled into this way of life war clouds began to gather. Food became scarce, coal was needed to keep the ammunition factories in production and prices shot up: eggs now cost one shilling (5p) each and white cotton two shillings (10p) per reel. There were serious health problems in England, including a severe influenza epidemic, malnutrition, consumption and pneumonia. Towards the end of the Great War my Mother presented Father with the son he had longed for. Alas, young John died at the age of six months. A short time afterwards, the youngest girls Phyllis and Margaret caught colds: pneumonia followed with complications and once more Father dug his hands deep into his pockets to pay for two more funerals.

By now Eva had left home to train as a Mental Nurse, Isobel had gone into service with the Plymouth family at nearby Hewell Grange and only Kathy was left at home, in poor health. Eighteen months later there was another funeral to pay for.

Eva finished her training in 1923 and I was told she became engaged to be married. She was referred to as a "big strapping lass", well built and just over 6ft tall. At this time, conditions in mental institutions were appalling. Food was poor and the working hours exceptionally long. Once more, fate stepped in. Eva contracted tuberculosis: there was no medicines available to keep her on this earth. She died six months after I was born.

By now Father had reached the end of his tether, not knowing which way to turn. Why had life struck him such a cruel blow'? He was middle aged, should have been enjoying his life and might have expected some grandchildren to bounce upon his knee. Instead, he was steeped in sorrow and unable to find an answer. He had never hurt anyone or even wished anyone any harm.

It was obvious that years of hard work, child-bearing and financial worry were wearing my Mother to a shadow. She was also very anaemic. "Just you eat plenty of raw liver: that will put the roses back into your cheeks". Alas, there was no treatment for

*My parents with their ill-fated family, circa 1910. Eva on the left and
Isobel in front of Father.*

pernicious anaemia and all the raw liver in the world wouldn't put those lovely roses back in my dear Mother's cheeks. Each day she became weaker and as the first rose slowly opened its petals to the early morning dew, she closed her weary eyes and quietly slipped away to a better land.

She had left behind a very sad and lonely man who wondered what on earth he was going to do with a three year old daughter.

"Don't thee fret theeself, John", remarked one of the canal navvies, "the runt of the litter 'er be; 'er won't be squaking fer long . . ."

It had always been quite obvious to me that my Father worshipped my Mother and when he lost his "Lassie", as he always called her, he wondered if he had anything left that was worth worrying about. Then he remembered that I must have been sent for some reason. But only God knew why.

Apart from Isobel, this is the family I do not remember. Left to right: Isobel, Kathy, Margaret, Phyllis and Eva. Just before the Great 'Flu Epidemic of 1917.

My parents had been through hell and poverty. Every crisis had been equally shared, but the biggest shock they ever received was the day I arrived.

It was long after I had learned the country way about the birds and the bees, climbing trees to watch the arrival of a new-born lamb . . . "pepping where you shouldn't be pepping" and had looked under the gooseberry bush that I learned the true story about my sharp and unexpected arrival on St Patrick's Day.

I was what was later termed in the medical profession as a BBA (Born Before Arrival). It seemed that my Mother had a sneaking suspicion that another baby might be due. But the family doctor said it was quite out of the question. No wonder I was referred to as "the scrapings of the pot". Scrapings of the pot indeed! they forgot to add that the sweetness is always at the bottom.

After the sad dark days of the Great War when one funeral seemed to follow another, my parents decided to try and push the past behind them and begin life anew. Late on the evening of March 16, 1924, Father was out attending to the back paddles, running off water in the expectation of a heavy storm. March had come in like a lamb but rough weather was now likely. Little did he realise when he went up to bed that here was a situation considerably more stormy than the one he had predicted outside.

My Mother quietly told him that she thought before the next morning there would be another mouth to feed.

"What are you babbling about, woman? The goat has had her kid."

"And I'm about to have mine", replied my Mother. "So pull your pants back on and get up that cut side to find a nurse from some-where."

By some strange coincidence, the nurse that arrived was Irish. The day was St Patrick's. And the violets were blooming on the reservoir bank.

"A child from nowhere", remarked Father. "With a name just ready and waiting. Patricia Violet it shall be."

When he had recovered from the shock, Father was able to add another song to his repertoire at the Halfway House: "Just because the violets are shining in the lane" became "Just because the violets were shining up the Cut . . ."

He always said my arrival would forever remain one of the sweet mysteries of life.

After my Mother died, my unmarried sister Isobel, who was

twenty years older than me, had to come home to keep house. I was approaching my fourth birthday when we first met. It was clear from the start that sparks would fly, for she was inclined to be rather bossy. When she ordered me to carry out some small task, I would retaliate and shout: "I'm not doing that, 'cause you're not my Mother!" The fact that I was the apple of my Father's eye didn't make the situation any easier. Times were hard, money was short and we had a struggle to get by.

It was a bitter blow for Isobel to have to come back to a cold and lonely place like Tardebigge with none of the little luxuries that helped to make life pleasant. Having a child to look after merely added to the hardships. She had been employed by a titled family in Scotland, was used to heating, lighting and running water, cooked with large solid fuel stoves, helped to entertain and had enjoyed free time to visit Scottish beauty spots such as Oban. She had always had plenty of company. To walk home late at night by the side of a Scottish loch was like heaven itself, compared with Tardebigge. The mist and the heather had become part of her life. There was no place on earth to match Scotland and she never tired of talking about it. I heard all about Loch Etive, Loch Awe, Ben Cruachan and Glen Etive long before I was five years old. I could picture the Scotsman in his swinging kilt and I knew what a sporran was. Every time I looked at the picture of the "Stag at Bay" which hung by the door at the bottom of the stairs, I imagined the deer in the forests standing very still, waiting and listening. And the sunlight streaming through the trees, casting a shadow of a large pair of antlers across the snowy woodland path.

All these stories of so many years ago must be the reason why I too love Scotland so much . . . and my porridge . . . even to this day.

Isobel was a small, thin woman, standing about 5ft 4ins; she had brown hair, a pale complexion and very long, thin fingers. She had sharp features, matched by a very sharp tongue. I was never forgiven for arriving so late in my Mother's life and she ruled me with a rod of iron. I felt that she regarded me as some form of freak of nature and decided that I would never be anything more to her life than a liability. My earliest recollections of my sister were very tearful and frightening, her manner cold and distant.

Isobel had once attended a fancy dress ball as Miss Muffet, wearing a very large stuffed black spider on her shoulder. this horrible thing would turn up in the least expected places and terrify the life out of me. Her secret fear was that Father might

A fairy on the Tardebigge Reservoir grounds, 1931.

remarry and she would be left with nothing. This possibility also worried me and the thought of the Princess and the wicked Stepmother often haunted me.

But bad dreams are soon forgotten. Tomorrow, once more, I would sit on my Father's knee and I would be his "Little Lassie", but to my sister, I would never be anything better than a "Holy Terror".

Many times I would hear old women say: "An only child's a lonely child. 'Er'll be olright when 'er gus ter school. You'll have 'er off yer hands then . . ." But I never was a lonely child. I had always been blessed with the most wonderful imagination; I had a dog, Tony and the little robin redbreast that perched on my Father's spade. He was my friend. The majestic heavy horses which pulled the canal boats all shared my secrets. And there were always the pictures in the fire . . . fairy castles and beautiful clouds. And I had swans, geese, rabbits and hedgehogs. I might have been lonely if I hadn't had so many feathered and furry friends.

Father began work at Tardebigge as a lock keeper in 1910 at an hourly rate of 1/3d (6.25p). Our cottage was "tied" so it was rent free; but it also meant that if you lost your job, you would be without a roof over your head. One advantage, however, was a free supply of coal every twelve months.

My Father was a well-built man with straight, dark hair, a small neat moustache and bushy eyebrows which partly concealed a pair of kind, twinkling dark brown eyes. Standing 5ft 10ins and weighing 15 stones, he was also a very strong man. The youngest but one in a family of six brothers and two sisters, he started work as a carter at the age of twelve, in 1891. He would set out from home at 4.30am, carrying a little penny candle in a lantern to light his way and walk the 9 miles from Tardebigge to King's Norton, work for a few days and retrace his weary steps home again. He was well liked by everyone, was very kind and thoughtful, and always had time to spare for others. For me, there was always time for a hug and a cuddle during the long working hours: always a shoulder to cry on.

He had a great store of "magic" potions to ease and relieve childish aches and pains. The only time in my early years that I ever suffered from earache was when a small boy held the explosive strip from a Christmas cracker and detonated it as close as possible to my ear. But kind words and warm "magic" drops were forthcoming and a warm, work-grimy, rough hand was

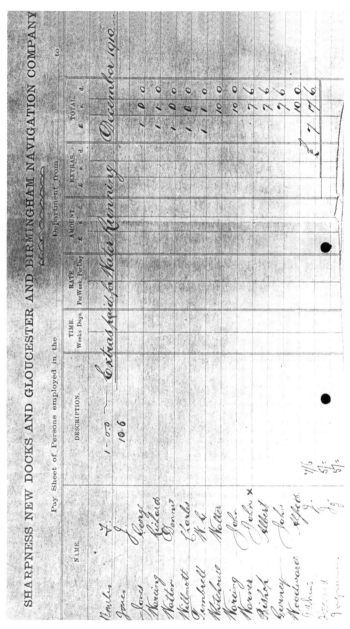

A *canal company wages sheet for December 1910. John Warner earned*
a bonus of 7/6d (37½p).

placed over my ear and very soon all tears and pain had vanished.

Father was an early riser, believing in getting up with the dawn chorus and closing his eyes at the setting of the sun, summer and winter alike. His first job was to light the burner on the oil stove to boil water for early morning tea. The remaining water would be used for shaving; we always washed in cold water! Father said this made you more alert. I preferred a "lick and a promise", especially on a winter's morning, when lumps of ice floated on top of the rain water bucket.

After drinking his tea, the next task would be to feed the livestock and to let the dog out of the kennel. Tony was a small black and white mongrel: a faithful little creature and my constant companion.

By the time I had toddled downstairs in my long flannelette nightdress, my feet would be almost frozen; but I would soon get them warm again by the cheerful fire which was always alight by 7 o'clock. Father made the porridge and toast and it was a great treat to sit with him to eat my breakfast. He wasn't very pleased the morning that I poked the fire with the handle of a tea knife, and I was rather puzzled as to why the handle had disappeared!

Father's working day began at 7am. He was responsible for the stretch of locks from the Engine House to the Halfway House. A daily record had to be kept of the rise and fall of water in the reservoir. This was done with a measuring post, sunk deep in the water and marked off at foot intervals. If heavy rain had fallen during the night, it might be necessary to "draw off" by winding up a small paddle on the top of the reservoir bank. This was similar to the lock paddles and was also operated with a windlass.

He could predict very early in the day what the weather would be like for the next 24 hours. He taught me which way the wind was blowing and how to tell the time from the position of the sun: watches were for the gentry only.

There are fifteen locks between the Engine House and the Halfway House, each measuring a little over 70ft in length, while each hill and pound between the locks is about 70 yards. It would be necessary to walk this distance a good many times each day, as well as crossing and re-crossing the locks repeatedly. The towing path was rough and stony, and although providing a good grip for the boat horses, it was very hard on our feet. But perhaps the stones were not as hard on Father's feet as was my darning: he wore long woollen socks and Isobel hated darning so much that from a very early age this became my job. Over his socks he wore stout leather leggings and a good strong pair of boots. He repaired all our shoes and would have made an excellent cobbler. His strong and rough clothes were topped with a heavy raincoat and on his head he wore a cap or trilby. Around his waist was a thick leather belt in which he carried his lock windlass. This same windlass had belonged to Great Grandad Warner and it is one of my most prized possessions.

There were two luxuries in Father's life: one was a glass of ale at the Halfway house and the other was his pipe of Digger Gold Flake. He could get a good many puffs from an ounce of 7½d (3p) tobacco.

Throughout his life he paid only three visits to the cinema. Two of the films were Charles Laughton as Henry VIII and Freddie Bartholomew as David Copperfield. Never ever did I hear him complain or grumble. He enjoyed his work and as each day dawned he would be seen setting about his tasks on the cut and puffing away at his pipe. As his work varied from day to day, it was

Father at work in the 1930s: with his windlass and dog Tony; carrying water at the lockside.

never likely to become monotonous. There were hedges to be cut with a hedging hook; ditches to be cleaned out; and the grass to be mown with a scythe. It was most important to keep a watchful eye on the condition of the wooden lock gates and to apply oil to the rack and pinion mechanism of the paddle gear. Due to the lock keeper's diligence in performing his duties, there was an air of well-being about the place.

During the 1930s, the cost of fishing permits which my Father issued for the Severn Fishery Board was one shilling (5p) per rod. If you needed a towpath permit for walking or cycling, they cost two shillings and sixpence (12½p) a year. Swimming in the canal was not encouraged; swimming in the reservoir was not allowed, for it was both very cold and dangerous.

One of Father's regular duties during the fishing season was to travel from home to Alvechurch to issue permits, normally on a Sunday morning. He would set out about 9am by foot or cycle and arrive back home at about 4pm, rather footsore and weary. I vividly recall one Sunday in 1932 when he came back so wet that I wouldn't have been surprised if little fishes had fallen out of his shoes. He greeted us with just two words: "I'm wet! "

"Wouldn't expect you to come home dry," replied Isobel, "It's been raining all morning. More than likely, your inside's wetter than your outside."

It came to light much later in the day that as he was cycling down the towpath under Cow Pasture Bridge, the front wheel of his cycle had hit a brick. Over the handlebars went Father, headfirst into the cut. This was about the third time that he had been in and once again he managed to retrieve his cap and his bicycle. I was amazed that he always managed to scramble out, as the water under the bridges was quite deep. He never did learn to swim.

I can still hear him saying "Don't poke the fire from the top" and "Don't help me to salt, or you'll help me to sorrow and I've had my share."

Other superstitions commonly mentioned were that a falling picture was a bad omen, for it meant that one would shortly hear of a death. And one of the biggest crimes in our home was to eat your food standing up. If you were to sing at the table, you would die in the Workhouse . . .

Tardebigge Parish Council allocated money from the rates to be distributed among the poor and needy. As I was "seen and not heard", Father's weekly wages were not discussed within my hearing, but at this time he was earning £1-17-6d (£1.87½p). These were the days when 3lbs of flour cost 11½d (4.8p); 2lbs of sugar, 6d (2½p); llb cocoa, 2/- (10p); llb of tea, 2/6d (12½p); ale, 7d per pint (2.9p); soap, 4d (1.7p); 400yds white cotton, 5½d (2.3p); and 20 cigarettes, 11½d (4.8p). After buying basic groceries for one week, there was precious little money to spare. There were no luxuries as bought cakes or "bloody rubbish", as Father described unnecessary trivialities.

Holidays were unheard up and Father never had one throughout his entire life. Often he would wonder where the next penny was to come from, but he maintained: "God's very good. If he doesn't call, he'll write." And this would probably mean a small win on the football pools, with a 3/6d (1 7 ½p) postal order in the post. Football was then very much the working man's game. On Saturday nights, he would sit glued to the earphones of the crystal set, concentrating on the results and waiting to see if his "draws had come off." During this traumatic period, I was not allowed to speak or move a muscle. But if he did win a little on the football, he would always remark: "Every day in every way, we get better and better and better."

Nothing would be wasted in these hard times. Feathers from poultry were baked in the oven and used for filling cushions and pillows. The large wing feathers made good pipe cleaners and were also very useful for applying oil to the lock paddle gear. All bones from the butcher or our own pigs were boiled for stock, while a very tasty meal could be made from a sheep's head and cow's heel. There was of course the odd occasion when one of the fishermen had a good day. If his family did not care for freshwater fish, that would take care of tomorrow's menu. My favourite fish was eel: those in the reservoir often weighed three or four pounds.

It was indeed fortunate that during my childhood we were healthy. Our family doctor could either come along the Tack Lane and then follow the road to the Engine House or via Grimley Lane and up Grimley Hill. If he chose the latter, he would leave his car at the Round Pound Bridge and walk almost a quarter of a mile along the towing path. Such calls to houses well off the beaten track must have been quite common. Doubtless he was very thankful that other families didn't have a horrible little girl like the one at the Warner's! Many years later, during my nursing career, I met our doctor again. He said he had often wondered why I had kicked him in the chest as he had lifted me onto the table to examine my throat. He was most thankful that I managed to get through the rest of my childhood without suffering the usual childish complaints.

In these tough times, 1d was paid each week into the Hospital Sunday Fund. Another 2d went into the Hewell Nursing Association Fund, entitling any member of the family to be nursed in their own home.

All the lock keepers' houses along the cutside were brick-built. There were three doors on the front of our house, all facing the canal. The front door was in the centre and protected by a wooden porch. At the end of the house looking up the cut was a door which led into the back kitchen. At the far end was the door leading into the shed, better known as "The Hovel". This was also brick-built and was used to store coal, wood, fruit, and fishing tackle. It was a warm, dark home for lots and lots of spiders. I was terrified of being in there if the wind blew the door closed, for the darkness was inky black.

Reservoir Cottage in 1919, with family and friends.

At the back of the house was a small built-on brick structure. Years before, it could have been a pig sty, but in my day it was known as "Dirty Dick's" and used for Father's distillery, where all his secret brewing took place.

A small lawn and flower garden were situated at each end of the house, while at the far end of the garden path, overlooking the reservoir, stood my haven of refuge – the closet, again built of brick. A low brick wall with rounded top ran along the front of the house as a safety precaution to prevent any overspill from the lock flooding our home. It didn't stop my bouncing ball from falling into the empty lock, or anything else which I might throw over'

Our cooking was done either in a twin-burner Valor oil stove or the old fashioned range on which we burnt coal and wood. It was necessary to be thrifty with the coal, for delivery was annual. Hence Father's motto: "Spare at the bag's mouth. It's not a bit of use trying to economise when you have only two lumps left to use."

Once a week, the oil man came in his van as near to the house as possible. Then, we were able to stock up with cans of oil, candles, matches, spare wicks for the lamps and perhaps also a spare globe for the Aladdin lamp. Cooking by oil could be disastrous: if you turned the wicks too high, great clouds of smoke billowed across the room and very soon the whole place was decorated with long black cobwebs. If the wicks were too low, the slightest breeze would put out the light. If they were set just right, the milk bubbled over the top of the saucepan, and the smell of burning lingered for days on end.

Ironing was a dramatic event. If you left the flat iron overnight in the oven at the side of the grate, it might be slightly warm the following morning. If you then tried heating it over the oil wick, by the time it was hot enough to use, it was also covered in a layer of black soot.

Our living room was always cosy, especially at night by the warm glow of the lamplight. A round table stood in the middle of the room and a long sofa beneath the window. Father's armchair was at one side of the table and various other small chairs were arranged here and there. Two long brass shell cases (relics of the First World War) stood in the hearth, one on each side of the fireplace where there was also a copper kettle. A large fireguard surrounded the old-fashioned black shiny range with its two hobs and small oven. This was polished with black lead and lots of "elbow grease". Another small living room adjoined this one, also with its own small range. There was no other method of heating the rest of the house.

Opposite the front door was a large and dark Welsh dresser, adorned with decorative plates. Father had built this outside in the "Hovel"; when it was finished, he had had to take it to pieces again to get it through the front door. After it had been in the house for less than a month, a lady called and offered him a "fair price" for it, thinking it was an antique!

The front door opened onto a small bricked yard with two steps leading up to the towing path. Ten feet further on was the edge of the lock chamber. When a boat passed through and the rush of water forced the double lock gates together with a bang, the plates and mugs on the dresser wobbled so much that they almost fell off.

One large china mug had an old country verse printed on its side:

God Speed the Plough
Let the wealthy and great
Roll in splendour and state.
I envy them not, I declare it.
I eat my own lamb, my chickens and ham
I shear my own fleece and I wear it.
I have lawns, I have bowers,
I have fruits, I have flowers.
The lark is my morning alarmer.
So jolly boys now,
Here's God, speed the plough.
Long life and success to the Farmer.

Beneath was the legend: "Industry Produceth Wealth".

A large cool pantry was situated underneath the stairs, its window overlooking the reservoir. Three stone steps led down to a brick floor, surrounded by thick stone slabs. On these shelves lay the sides of bacon while being cured. It was also an ideal place to keep 20lb blocks of salt as well as butter, which would otherwise have turned to oil during the hot summer days.

In the winter when a good strong gale howled across the reservoir, it was quite impossible to keep out the draughts which moaned and groaned under the pantry door and lifted the linoleum right off the floor. A boundary line ran through the centre of the pantry: if you were on the bacon side, you were in Tardebigge. But if you were putting groceries in the meat safe on the other side, you were in Stoke Prior. So cold was it in here that during the winter the eggs would freeze almost solid, each one developing a hair-line crack. Milk jugs were covered with small, round, muslin mats with tiny coloured beads stitched around the edge to hold them in position.

One big cupboard fixed high up on the pantry wall away from inquisitive little fingers contained a "salve for every sore". Things like the small, clean glass bottle whose neck was placed in hot water and held over the head of a boil; this was only used if a bread poultice failed. A jar of powdered Alum was a sure cure for mouth ulcers. Oil of Eucalyptus for colds. Camphorated oil for rubbing on chests, or goose grease from a jar. Coughs were treated with a mixture of butter, sugar, milk, honey and cinnamon. Alternatively, we took tea brewed from blackcurrant leaves. Tummy aches were given a good dose of Oil of Peppermint, sometimes followed by Senna Pod tea or Syrup of Figs. After a helping of either, you wouldn't dare to cough! Tincture of Iodine was for cuts . . . anywhere, any place. Parsley was for bladder troubles. All bruises and sprains were treated with a Horse Linament or Embrocation, a mixture of turpentine, linseed oil and neatsfoot oil with the warning to keep away from the fire and a good distance away from other people.

Oil of cloves and Tincture of Myrrh were soothing for toothache. Linseed Meal was also used as a poultice, while Camomile Flowers infused in boiling water gave some relief for inflammation. Turpentine, beeswax and resin were kept for making furniture and French polish. And then, there was always a little tin of Union Jack corn paste.

The only concoction I really enjoyed swallowing was a cure-for-all-ills called Mulled Ale. This was a mixture of eggs, milk and nutmeg, made into what looked like a very runny egg custard. When cool, it was beaten into a quantity of ale from the barrel. To my tiny mind it tasted better than Syrup of Figs and had almost the same effect.

Most of the basic groceries were purchased from Ten Acres & Stirchley Co-operative Society. Between 2/6d (12½p) and 3/6d (17½p) a week went on such items as tea, sugar, margarine, flour, oatmeal, matches, soap and the odd items which varied from week to week. These included dried pulses, dried fruit, rice, sago, tapioca and the never-to-be-forgotten caraway seeds for Father's favourite cake. You shopped at the Co-op to save stamps for the annual "Divvy".

I enjoyed my visits to the Co-op, the main attraction being the method by which money was directed to the cash office. An assistant placed the customer's money into a small wooden cup which was screwed into a lid; this was attached to a cable running overhead from the counter to the cash office at the far end of the shop. As soon as the money was safely placed inside, the assistant pulled a lever on the cable and cup and contents shot through the air to be delivered to the cashier. On arrival, the container would be unscrewed, filled with any change and a receipt, put back into place and then . . . ping went the lever and back to the customer came the contents. Such a method of cash delivery to a central pay box was called the Lampson System, or Lampson Dart.

I delighted in watching the grocer packing sugar into dark blue bags, folding the tops over with expertise. Back at home, when these bags were emptied, they were carefully flattened out and taken to the coal shed to be packed with slack, their tops being once more folded just as they had been in the shop. The resulting coal bricks would make our fuel supplies last a little longer.

Some winter evenings, I would dress up in my warmest clothes, Father would light the hurricane lamp and we sat in the old coal shed or "Hovel", busily wrapping apples and pears in paper to make them store better. This fruit would keep for months and fill the house with a lovely aroma. The pears were Father's pride and joy; known as "Marguerites", they were huge and juicy and often weighed 17ozs or more. They were so big that the tree branches had to be supported with thick props. A net thrown over the top kept the birds away.

Father always had plenty of outside jobs to do. These included fetching the logs and coal in to last the long evenings, trimming the wicks for the oil lamp, chopping firewood and making sure that the poultry was safe. When all the doors were closed and locked, a cosy fire burning in the range and the lamp was lit, Father would change into his slippers, sit in his armchair, light his pipe and say: "Nothing on this earth will move me from this chair tonight."

But as sure as God made little apples, a small voice would say: "Dad, I want to go to the lavatory."

"Are you sure?"

"Yes, Dad."

"Well, go on. Take the lamp."

"No. You come with me. There might be some spiders and it's a long way up the garden path."

"You little varmint. Why didn't you say, before I took my shoes off?"

To get to our lavatory on a winter's evening was like preparing to climb Mount Everest. You were made to dress up in warm clothes and undress when you arrived. Inside the small brick building with its squeaky door were two wooden seats. A big one and a little one. Toilet paper was only for the very rich. The daily newspaper and *Old Moore's Almanack* would be tied on a string and hung on the back of the door. As you sat on the wooden "throne", the wind would howl through the trees and the water would lap against the wall at the back of the house. Similarly, the waves in the canal would splash against the coping stones along the edge of the lock at the front. Now and again, the owls would hoot and a vixen would scream. All just a little bit frightening, when you are not yet five years of age.

Four Warner brothers at Lock 53 in about 1945. Left to right: Father, John Warner; Harry Warner from Coventry; Will Warner, keeper of Tardebigge Top Lock; and Sam Warner, the policeman from Ombersley.

The winter nights at Tardebigge were very, very long. I well remember that sometimes the snow would start before Christmas and continue until March or April. The light faded very rapidly and darkness was upon you by 4pm. I hated to go upstairs alone, for it was weird and creepy. The grownups said: "Someone has died in the small bedroom . . . and someone has died on the stairs . . . and of course, you know, her mother died in that back bedroom, didn't she? Poor woman, God rest her soul!" I would be made to go upstairs and fetch things and I was so petrified that I sang loudly and thought that my lungs would burst.

"You'll catch it, our Pat, when you come down. Kicking up that racket. Just how long does it take you to go upstairs? I suppose you've been gazing at yourself in the mirror again." What they didn't know was that I stood before the mirror with my eyes tightly closed, then tried to peep through my eyelids to see if I could find out what I looked like if I were dead!

"Stop rushing up and down those stairs," shouted Father. "Anyone would think the Devil himself was chasing you. One of these days you'll come such a cropper. And pay attention when I talk to you." And a meek little voice answered: "Yes, Father."

Fortunately, Nature had a way of providing us with her own brilliant light. At certain times of the year the "Parish Lamp" shone through the bedroom window, illuminating the room to such an extent that it was possible to see to read. I would gaze through the window and see the face of the Man in the Moon, which always held a great fascination for me. If you looked across the reservoir on a night when the moon was full, everything would be quiet and still with not a ripple on the water nor even a wave lapping against the bank. Only the beautiful face of the moon, laughing up at you from out of the water.

Almost the first words of wisdom I recall from my Father were: "Your fortune's great . . . if you don't work, you don't ate." He was a mine of information and never once said "I don't know". And heaven knows, I asked enough questions.

Often he would read the tea leaves in the bottom of the cup; maybe it was sheer good luck, but quite frequently many of the things he predicted came true. He was not a deeply religious man, but a Christian through and through, always helping those in need. God knows, we were poor, yet there always seemed to be some unfortunate soul far worse off than we were.

Father's motto was "If you can't do anyone a good turn, then for Heaven's sake don't do them a bad one. "And he would say:

"Always pay for what you have and never be beholden to anyone. Always stay independent."

Many times I have seen him fill a basin with a good helping of hot stew, place a saucer on top and then tie them up in a tea towel to keep warm. Then off he would go, facing all winds and weathers to take the meal to some individual even less fortunate than we were. It was never too much trouble. He would look so old and weary, but then, of course, to me he was always old.

There were many times in his life when he was utterly bewildered as to why fate had been so unkind to him after the early happy days of his marriage. To lose everything that he had worked so hard for was something that he never did understand. Family sorrows were never discussed when I was around and I was too young to comprehend why, at certain times, my Father was so sad. Our home was filled with sadness: little treasures and trinkets tucked away in boxes and drawers . . . a hair slide, a faded photograph, a hymn book, a neatly folded hand-embroidered handkerchief. Some of them were wrapped in tissue paper, now old and creased, but much too dear to part with.

As I lay in bed at night, little whispers and sounds filled every corner of the room. When all was quiet downstairs, the house seemed to come alive. During the day, my young ears had caught snatches of muffled conversation from relatives and casual callers. People would talk, babbling on, thinking I was not listening. Someone said: "Agnes had a beautiful voice" and it made me think that maybe it *was* my mother I heard singing last night. Many times I would hear one of my dead sisters crying on the stairs in the dark. It must have been Margaret, for I had heard she had once fallen down there. Listen! What's that I can hear? Someone tapping on the window. It's Kathy trying to get in! I remembered hearing that Mother had spanked her and put her to bed early one night; and she had climbed out through the window and escaped down the Virginia Creeper . . . she must be trying to get back in . . . I wouldn't climb down that: it's full of spiders.

Now I can hear a fox or maybe its a screech owl. If I shout loud enough Father will come upstairs and tell me a story. He knows lots of stories and some of them are true. He's a great storyteller: I like the one about the ice and the cut. That's my favourite. "Dad-d-d, tell me a story about the ice . . ." And so he began . . .

It wasn't the first time I had heard this one and it certainly wouldn't be the last. Many times he had built my castles in the air and captured my imagination and this story I knew word for word.

The winter of 1916–17 was the worst freeze-up ever recorded on the Worcester & Birmingham Canal. It was frozen from King's Norton to Worcester for nine long weeks, with the ice remaining between 18 inches and two feet thick. The oil-engined tug *Sharpness* ran the stretch between King's Norton and Worcester Bar, Birmingham, night and day, attempting to break open a way for the coal boats whose deliveries were so desperately needed. This was a crucial time for the country in the middle of the Great War and it was essential to keep the factories supplied. They were then steam powered and would have been forced into closure if the coal supplies had stopped. Factories such as King's Norton Paper Mills, the King's Norton Brick Company and Cadbury Bros at Bourneville.

With such appalling weather conditions it was not even possible to send the coal by horse and cart and anyway this would have helped little with the enormous quantities required. The men on the ice-breaking gang were faced with a terrible ordeal, for just how do you get a small wooden ice boat moving when it is stuck fast in a solid mass of ice two feet thick?

After several weeks of total stoppage, almost like a miracle the sun forced its way through the clouds and as the day wore on the temperature rose a few degrees. A gentle thaw set in and as the men boarded the ice-breaker, they felt a slight movement beneath their feet. At last they could make a start. Every available man was pressed into service to face the great challenge that lay ahead.

On the first day, with the help of twelve heavy horses, they navigated from Worcester to Stoke Prior, rocking the boat from side to side to break the ice into massive chunks. The going was hard: their clothing was far from adequate and few wore gloves. With steel windlasses to handle at the locks and the metal rails covered in ice, their bare fingers would stick, often removing patches of skin. And this was just the first day.

The following morning, if anything, it got even worse. They were starting to climb up to Tardebigge from "the foot of the thirties" at Stoke Prior. Two extra horses were brought in to help. Father said that this was the greatest number he had ever seen used on the canal. Cold, hungry, footsore and weary, the men and beasts finally arrived at Tardebigge through sheer guts and determination. On the third day, they left Tardebigge Wharf with ten horses and arrived at King's Norton just as dusk was falling. It was a tremendous ordeal for everyone concerned. But little was the thanks they got; or the money or food. These men were tough

The ice-boat above Lock 53, circa 1928.

Looking across the lock to the pig sty, circa 1928.

and they had achieved what they had set out to do. The end of the journey was their only reward.

There were no flags or bunting flying, no crowds to cheer them. Just a wonderful sense of satisfaction within their hearts and memories to treasure till the day they died. For many months afterwards as Father lay down to sleep, he could still hear the mens' voices calling out "Whoa, Gee-up, Drop that paddle, Mind that rope." Still hear the horses' hooves slipping in the ice and snow; still smell the warm sweat from their straining bodies and see the hot breath which streamed from their nostrils and hit the cold frosty air like a thick fog.

After a well-earned rest, a chunk of bread and cheese and a swig of tea, the men began to prepare for their return journey. By now the horses were well rested and stood quietly munching away at their chaff, their faces buried deep in large canvas nose bags. They were much too occupied to notice the head collars and tackle being brought out for use again.

But they knew that somewhere along the journey another cosy stable would shelter them from the cold winter air and that like their masters they would return in the same manner as they had come: on foot.

Ice breaking, 1928.

Most winters the stretch of canal from the house to the school would freeze solid, preventing the boats moving from lock to lock. And the ice-boat would be put to use. This was a long, somewhat oval, round-bottomed vessel with a mast at each end and a bar running down the centre. Four men would stand on the wooden deck, grip the bar and rock the boat from side to side as it crashed along, drawn forward by horses on the towpath. Sometimes it would ride up onto the ice; occasionally, it would rock so far that it seemed as if it must go under. For me, a ride on the ice-boat was a great treat.

In cold weather, it was constantly in use, keeping the ice broken from day to day and so preventing it from forming into a solid mass. Normally drawn by one or two heavy horses or a pair of mules, donkeys would also sometimes be used. I loved the donkeys. They were such appealing creatures, with sad faces. They reminded me of Palm Sunday and Christ's triumphant ride into Jerusalem. I remembered the closing lines of G K Chesterton's *The Donkey:*

<blockquote>
There was a shout about my ears,
And palms before my feet.
</blockquote>

Only I always altered "palms" to "snow".

Our lock in mid-Winter, circa 1930.

CHAPTER TWO

The Special Days

THE MOST wonderful event of all was the arrival of Bromsgrove Fair, Horse Fair and Fun Fair combined. Fair Day was June 24, the same day for digging the first of the new potatoes. The Fair belonged to Pat Collins and one year a large number of horses and ponies were brought to the field near our house. Some of the animals strayed onto the towpath. Fortunately, Father was able to round them up, so it was free rides and all the Fun of the Fair for the Warner family.

It was a most memorable occasion: the huge roundabout of big wooden horses, over the sticks, the bumper cars, swing boats, boxing booths, the cake walk and the wall of death. But my most exciting moment was the sight and sound of the great musical monster which emitted a most wonderful noise. I stood and gazed at this magnificent array of pipes, drums, statues, figure heads sprouting angels' wings, cymbals and coloured lights. This was the Wonderland, the unforgettable Pat Collins Fair Organ, made by C H Marenghi & Co, Paris. How did they manage to get this all the way from Paris?

The magnificent Pat Collins Fair Organ.

Bromsgrove Horse Fair was held on the Recreation Ground at the back of the town. As I lay in bed at night, following my visit, I could hear strains of music drifting across the fields on the still, warm summer air. The summer nights could be very hot, and I needed to cover myself with only a sheet. I could also hear the big stamping hammer thumping away at Garrington's factory at Aston Fields.

The journey to Bromsgrove was by "hoof". The bus fare was 5d (2p), but we couldn't afford this so "Pat, my lass, you must hoof it!" It was a long walk down the four locks of the canal to Grimley Lane, along Tack Lane into Aston Fields and all the way along the New Road, until, phew, we finally arrived in Bromsgrove. There was a short cut across Finstall Park, but even that was a long way and not to be considered if the bull was around!

Country miles are always much longer than town miles, especially when you only have little legs. By the time we had walked down the canal to the Round Pound Bridge and along Grimley Lane which ran nearly in line with the cut, we were practically back where we started. I wished and wished . . . if only Dixon's Plantation (opposite our house) had just a teeny weeny path through it, we would have got there in half the time. Recently, I travelled this way by car and was amazed at the miles I used to cover. No wonder my legs ached! Sometimes on these long walks my Sister would accuse me of not having had a wash. So I would be given one in a puddle or a brook. It wasn't that I was dirty: I just used to dry a bad colour.

We might call at my Aunt's house in Wellington Road, the home of the Crumpton family. There were plenty of luxuries there: small jars of Marmite, Camp Coffee, Daddies Sauce. And Swiss Roll *and* cakes for tea. Aunt Muriel had two girls, Betty and Vivienne and a lovely Chow dog. Uncle Harold, my Aunt's husband, was my Mother's only brother.

My Sister would say: "Now listen to me, our Pat. You will have one cake or one piece of Swiss Roll. Not both." But she didn't know that Aunt Muriel had a soft spot for me and also knew that I had a passion for Swiss Roll. So she first handed me a cake and then insisted I finished up with a nice big slice of Swiss Roll.

"You spoil the kid. She won't eat it, you know. There you are, I told you so! I knew she couldn't finish it. I told you, our Pat, before we came out to say 'No Thank You' if you were offered another slice of cake. Trouble with you is your eyes are bigger than your belly."

My Sister would go on and on, and one thing would always be included: "I think that it was dreadful that my Mother" (never *our* Mother) "should have a child at *that* age. After all, I had to come home and look after her." Little did she realise that I would grow up to be one of the wonders of the universe!

Shopping excursions always ended in disaster. I either got lost or everything I looked at collapsed around my ears. The slogan of Woolworths was "Nothing over sixpence (2½p) in the store." If ever I went to buy an article for 6d, my money was invariably handed back by the assistant because it had turned out to be a silver 3d bit!

I enjoyed the walk to Bromsgrove provided that I wasn't wearing new shoes. But blisters or not, I didn't dare complain, for my shoes were generally second hand; if I was lucky enough to have new ones I would remember "pride must always have a pinch."

From dusk until dawn, the long night hours were filled with weird sounds. Maybe it was a rat jumping off the coping stones which suddenly went "plop". Or a hungry fox sniffing around the edge of the lock, hoping to find a morsel to eat, or having picked up the scent of a rabbit or cock pheasant.

The lock outside the house was left empty at night and in times of storm the water would lap against the gates. The gates themselves would creak and groan. Lots of strange noises, but nothing to be afraid of . . . just the echoes from the empty lock.

One very dark and stormy night, when the wind howled and the rain battered against the window panes, we were sitting in the lamplight by the cosy fire when suddenly heavy footsteps were heard outside. "Who is there?" shouted Father. Then came a knocking, followed by a man's voice, asking for help. Upon opening the door, Father was amazed to find an airman. He explained that owing to the terrible storm he had been forced to land his small bi-plane in a field at the side of the next lock down the canal. The man spoke with a German accent. The year was 1930. After Father had checked the airman's credentials, he was given a meal and shelter for the night.

One great episode in my young life would be the delivery by boat of a year's supply of coal. This would take a whole day because there was no machinery available and everything was moved by hand. This coal was part of Father's wages. A massive pair of scales would be wheeled from the boat and before anything else happened I would have to stand on the platform to check my weight. Would you believe it? I could get blacker than the men who handled the coal. Still, why worry? We were surrounded by water, so there was no excuse for not having a wash.

I can still hear a boatman's gruff voice echoing in my ears: "Git art o' there, you grubby little criter."

From start to finish, coal sorting could take two to three days. There was more than five tons to handle and stack, each lump weighing between thirty and forty pounds. At last the boat would be empty and the boatman would be putting on his jacket, ready to depart.

"Stop follerin' me around, young Pat. I knows what you be askin' me and answer's No."

"Please, Mister."

"No!"

"Please, Mister. Only a little ride."

"No!"

"Please, Mister. Only to the next lock."

"Thee'll git theesel' filthy."

"Don't matter."

Imagine a ride up the cut in an empty coal boat. All nice and black and me, with my best white socks on! As the boat rose level with the lock side, out of the bottom of the empty hold scrambled a little urchin. Black as the Ace of Spades, but oh, so happy.

"Thanks, Mister. Ta ta."

Away I went, skipping along and singing. Not a care in the world. These happy carefree days would never come again and it was such a treat to have a ride in a canal boat.

After the Lord Mayor's Show comes the muck-cart. Greetings from Isobel . . . wait for it!

"Where, in the name of Creation have you bin to get into that state?"

"Up the cut in the coal boat!"

"Don't tell fibs. You've got that expression from your Father. Just look at your socks and your knees! And it's no use spittin' on your hanky, thinking it will clean it off."

"Don't matter. Anyway, it's true. I have bin up the cut in a . . ."

"Don't tell such stories. Your Father only says that when a nosey little criter like you wants to know where he's going and he can't take you with him."

Actually, this was one of Father's favourite expressions, used when he was off to collect his meagre wages or if he was going for a drink at the Halfway House late at night. Otherwise, he would frequently say:

Playing shop, 1927.

Teddy Bears Picnic with Hilda Jones from Bournville, 1931.

"I'm going to see a man about a dog."
These expressions were only used to satisfy my curiosity.

Another great event was Pig Killing. Down the towpath would walk the butcher, armed with his Humane Killer and a selection of long knives. He would be followed by a gang of merry men, the local lads, all anxious for a little bit of pig meat in lieu of payment. After a puff on their pipes and a few glasses of Father's homemade wine, they really were merry men! Sometimes they didn't know whether they were handling a pig or feathering a turkey. I would try to hide and stuff my ears to keep out the noise of the pig's squeals. One year, I thought I would let the pig out before the butcher arrived and we would run away together. Poor Pig! He fell into the cut and nearly ended up in a watery grave.

This annual ritual took place in March or April. Pork was only eaten when the month contained an R, so all the meat left over was salted down for use later. The pig was the poor man's treasure, his most prized possession. His meat, bacon and fat supply for the long, hard winter months which lay ahead.

After the butcher and his mates had sampled Father's homemade wine again, I would stand and gaze at poor Pig, slung up on a hook, with a large white veil called the Kell, over his face. Poor Pig! Never again would he grunt at me as I tossed him my apple cores (the ones I wasn't allowed to throw in the fire). Never again would I scratch his back as I swung on the door of the sty. "Don't suppose I'll be allowed near the sty again. Not after that little episode early this morning!"

"I won't eat any more bacon. So there! Nor any faggots. Or lard. Or boney pies. Or chitter . . ."

"Well, my lass. You'll go to bed very hungry."

When the pig had been appropriately jointed, the sides of bacon would be put down to salt and the "leaf" (fat) rendered down. The fat was then poured into basins with sprigs of rosemary floating on top. This was the lard to spread on our toast for tea in the winter time as we sat in the lamplight. I might get a pocketful of "scratching" if I hung around: small lumps of cold, roasted fat. I didn't like them, but the birds did and so did my dog Tony!

Next, would come the faggot-making, followed by the boney pies. Even the head and tail were used to make brawn. The biggest task of all was cleaning the "belly". The intestines were washed and soaked in a large zinc bath. Then Father stripped off long willow sticks and these were used to turn the chitterlings inside out. The very long ones were plaited, soaked in brine, well rinsed and finally boiled in a large pot. They were surprisingly tasty. Anyhow, it was a case of eat what you are given or go without.

Once a year during the summer months, my "Christmas" Aunt and Uncle from Wolverhampton would come to stay.

"Here's our Polly coming down the cut, complete with all her pills and potions."

Father's words never altered. It was always the same statement every year.

After my Aunt had unpacked, I sat on the bed and stared at the

School photo, 1935.

wonderful array which had emerged from her small suitcase. It was carefully displayed on the bedside chair: the Bowel Controller's Paradise! What a good thing it was for me that labels advising "Keep all medicines out of the reach of children" had not been heard of. Goodness me! What a selection! They must have cost an awful lot of money. Now, let me see . . . I can play shops with this lot.

Beecham's Pills, Do-Do Tablets (for breathing problems), Bile Beans, Carter's Little Liver Pills, Juniper Pills, Glauber Salts (like Epsom Salts), Milk of Magnesia, Bismuth Powder, Germolene Ointment, Fuller's Earth Powder, Odol Toothpaste and an assortment of bottles of Cough Linctus. It would have been impossible to ask for the wrong thing: something to make you "go", and if you "went" too much, something to make you "stop"! A good dose of salts at night would guarantee a "flying start" to the day. First one past the sweet peas gets the best seat! If you didn't suffer from wind before you started taking all these pills, you would be certain to have a really good attack of it at some time during the next 24 hours.

Even Father was intrigued by the Odol Toothpaste. We always cleaned our teeth with soot or salt, so, thinking this was a dental fixative that he had heard about, he decided to squeeze a large amount onto his top plate. Little did he anticipate how hot it was!

I suppose that the part of my Aunt's visit which delighted me more than anything, was the unusual items of food she brought. Each time she came with a selection of delicious luxuries: a tin of salmon, a large tin of fruit salad swimming in sweet juice, and a large thin-necked bottle of sterilized milk. This milk packed in a bottle was a great novelty. I had only ever tasted milk from a milk-can or in a glass, fresh from the cow. I couldn't fathom how the milk had got into the bottle. I only knew that in those days I thought it was simply delicious. I finally arrived at the conclusion that town cows produced their milk all neatly packed in bottles!

The other luxuries were kept for Sunday Tea. The small tin of salmon made such tasty little sandwiches, so much nicer than bread and lard. I dressed myself up in my best bib and tucker and after devouring a lovely tea of salmon sandwiches and fruit salad which made me feel like Alice in Wonderland, we set out to walk to a tiny dot on the map called Woodgate, not far from Dodderhill Common. It was off down the cut, across the fields, past Patchett's Farm, through the long meadow and down a very steep hill. In the spring, this hill was a carpet of primroses and cowslips.

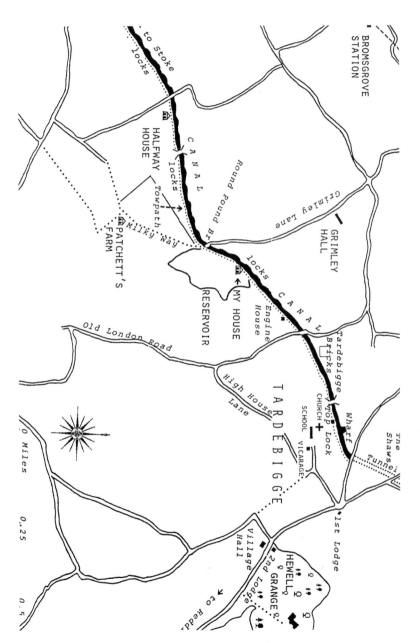

Tardebigge and surrounding area.

Sometimes we gathered armfuls of cowslips for wine-making, as this was one of Father's specialities.

In the early summer this same hill was blanketed with blue-bells. The scent and colour was quite breathtaking! The sun shone, the birds sang, the air was clean and fresh. Everything about this magical place made you glad to be alive. From the nearby woods came the call of a jay, the gentle coo-ing of a wood pidgeon and, if you were lucky, the song of the nightingale. I wandered along, holding Father's hand and gazed upward to watch a lark hovering overhead. I became so engrossed in the wonders of the Universe that I completely lost track of the miles that my little legs had covered. Finally, the end of the journey would come in sight and a 1d (0.4p) glass of pop would make it all worth while. This was bought at The Gate Hangs Well. The wooden seat outside was most welcome rest for hot, tired and footsore travellers. The local farmers gathered here for a swig and a chat on a Sunday evening.

The sign over the front entrance read:

"This gate hangs well to no man's sorrow. Pay today and trust tomorrow."

It was a long way to walk just to wet your whistle. But then, there was nothing much else to do.

The seasons of the year seemed to be sharply defined. After the hard winters with ice and snow, the birds suddenly started to sing, the snowdrops appeared, followed by wild violets, catkins hung in the hedges and great displays of pussy willow or palm appeared near the water's edge. At this time of the year the Canada Geese arrived. Together with the swans everything in the garden really was lovely. There were so many different things to see and it didn't cost a farthing.

Summertime was beautiful. It was daylight until after 10.00pm, often quite hot and sultry with terrific thunder storms. But once the storms had passed, the following days would be just as hot as before.

Along came Autumn, with all its wonderful hues: beautiful browns and golds. But it was always the saddest part of the year, making me acutely aware of the long winter ahead. There was the task of picking pounds and pounds of blackberries to make the delicious bramble jelly that graced our tea table. I liked picking blackberries but hated the briars and thorns that wrapped their tentacles around my legs and socks.

At certain times of the year we were very short of water. It could be a great problem: other times, there was too much! A drought was always a good excuse for not having had a wash! If the water in the cut ran low, the boats were brought to a complete standstill. And the reservoir would be full of fish lying stranded on the mud and gasping for breath. Washing days became really difficult. The soft water butts were empty and the nearest alternative supply of drinking water was too far to carry much. If the spring which fed the well beneath the pump also ran low, we were faced with a real life drama.

Clothes washing would entail dipping water from the canal, using a bucket on a length of rope. Thus, we were able to fill the old "copper" or "furnace" (as it was sometimes called). A good fire soon roared underneath the copper, and as the water came up to boiling point we were able to skim off the scum which by now floated on top in large lumps. It looked a bit like the froth on Tommy Thompson's ale. The water was by now reasonably clean, although it still smelled a bit fishy. My Sister had not had much experience with washing, so consequently her results were sometimes disastrous.

The greatest washing day drama occured the week before Christmas 1929. Father had scraped together all his odd pennies to treat himself to some new underwear, long overdue. One pair of long woollen underpants with a short-sleeved woollen vest to

Father feeding swans on the Reservoir by our house.

match. It was customary to wash any new items of underwear before putting them on: this removed any chemical substances. Well, Father insisted that his new underwear should duly be washed. So, into the hot, soapy water they landed. Each time Sister tried to lift them out with the "dolly stick" they went sliding around the copper, just like a great mass of frog spawn. Round and round the copper they swam. And round went the dolly stick after them.

Eventually, after the blue air had escaped through the scullery window (and most of the steam with it) a final attempt brought success. "Plop" went the wet, soggy mass that had been Father's new underwear. Oh, good shot! They landed in the bucket first attempt. Then, out of the bucket into the icy cold water to be rinsed, through the old wooden mangle and out onto the clothes line. Here, they were pegged out in the frosty air, soon to become as stiff as a ramrod.

They were so stiff when they were brought indoors that each garment stood upright like a suit of armour . . . and it wasn't due to the fact that they were frozen.

"Never mind" said Sister. "Don't you dare tell your Father. He won't notice if you keep quiet."

Three days later, we all began to prepare for our Christmas journey to Wolverhampton. Suddenly, an apparition in the shape of Father appeared on the landing.

"What the —— have you done to my new pants and vest?" he roared.

It was a real sight to see. I thought it was Father Christmas without his cloak. There stood Father, unable to bend. He looked as though he had been poured into his underclothes, stiff as a board and very, very shrunk. Every time we changed buses on the journey from Tardebigge to Wolverhampton, Father made straight for the nearest lamp post, furiously rubbing his back in the hope of getting a little relief.

Washing the blankets was great fun and was only attempted during warm weather. The bath was filled with warm, soapy water. In went the blankets, off came my shoes and socks and in I went, up to my ankles. Then it was tread, tread, tread. As soon as the blankets looked clean enough, they were rinsed and hung on the line.

Friday night was bath night. Once more, the old copper was filled and a good fire encouraged to roar underneath. I loved to sit in the round hip bath in the candle light. The warm glow from the fire made my cheeks burn, although at the same time my back froze from the cold north wind which howled and whistled through the gap at the bottom of the door, bringing the rain in with it. I imagined I was sailing in an old tub in the face of a Force Ten.

It took a long time to remove all the undergarments I was obliged to wear: long woollen stockings, thick woolly drawers, liberty bodice, combinations and a vest. The liberty bodice had lots of buttons up the front. I wasn't allowed to take it off over my head, as it would have pulled out of shape. I must undo every button. This was a long-lasting problem. I thought and thought and at last worked out a plan where I was able to take off my "combs" without removing the bodice. Then I would be able to sleep in it without all the trouble of those buttons. Well, I did think that I might get away with it!

I had a swing on the plum tree, quite near to the edge of the reservoir. Some days, I would sit with a stick, a piece of string and a bent pin and fish for hours. The water at this point was very shallow. After Father had fished me out for at least the seventh time, he came to the conclusion that I must be like a cat and had been blessed with nine lives.

We had a Crystal Set radio with two sets of ear phones. You had to tickle the "Cat's Whisker" to pick up a station. We would sit in the lamplight, Father wearing one set of ear phones and Sister and I holding an ear phone a-piece. I could listen in to the Children's Hour with Uncle Mac, and hear *Toytown* with Larry the Lamb and Ernest, the Policeman. There would be Henry Hall and his Danceband and *In Town Tonight*. We also had an old His Master's Voice gramophone with a huge trumpet. The picture on the front showed a little terrier dog, sitting with his ear to the horn. Wind the handle, put a new needle in the "sound box" and we had our

The Crystal Set.

Our His Master's Voice gramophone.

own music. My favourite records were *The Fairy Dreamboat*, John McCormack singing *The Trumpeter and the Old House* and a bit of jazz, such as *I met her in Monteray*. *The Trumpeter* was on a huge thick 78, recorded on one side only.

In the evenings, father would read to me: *Grimms' Fairy Tales*, *The Basket of Flowers*, and *A Peep Behind the Scenes*. This last one was a very sad story about a circus and fairground family. Dickens' stories were always popular. I liked jigsaw puzzles and Tiddlywinks. I became a member of the Nig Nogs and also the *Daily Mail's* Teddy Tail League. They sent me a birthday card on March 17 every year.

Birthday presents were generally scarce: a little book, a new comb, a fancy hair slide or length of ribbon. I might be able to buy Father a ld (0.4p) packet of matches or spills. Perhaps for Isobel a hair net or a packet of hair grips. I still have a few picture postcards which came on my birthday. Some have photographs of Shirley Temple and Gladys Cooper, both known during this period as "heart throbs". On the back, they have ld stamps.

Easter Sunday morning was exciting, because we had pink boiled eggs for breakfast. It was many years before I discovered that the water in which they had been boiled was coloured with cochineal. This was the end of the Lenten Fast, during which everyone was expected to give up some small luxury. I thought it a good idea to give up using soap. But no-one else seemed to agree with me.

Once one of the fishermen's wives gave me a lovely doll's pram made out of cane and a beautiful china doll, which I called Katy. I was allowed ld-worth of sweets each week. Once they were eaten, there would be none until the following week. Later on, I

A postcard saved from my First Birthday and very typical of designs in circulation during the 1920s. Below: reverse of another card, given me by Father. His writing shows confidence for a man who received so little formal education.

Back and front of the card received from the Teddy Tail League on my 12th birthday. Note the postage rate: ½d!

was able to have *The Chicks Own* comic and *The Children's Newspaper.* I became the proud owner of a whip and top and was even fortunate enough to have a Yo-yo. I felt very rich.

Tony, my black and white mongrel was a faithful little soul and din't mind having his leg in a sling or a bandage on his tail. I could also push him around in the doll's pram. He was often the subject of conversations between Father and the boat people.

"What breed be 'e, then John? Ain't seen one like that afore."

Father's answer was always the same:

"Well, I should say he's a cross between a bull and a window shutter."

Once, just once, I was taken out to dinner.

This was an outing to Uncle Sam's at Ombersley, near Worcester. He was a Police Sergeant and lived at the Police Station. I was given the usual warning to be on my best behaviour. In other words, to be seen and not heard. My Aunt and Uncle had three sons and two daughters, so there was quite a gathering at the dinner table. All was well and I remained seen but not heard until:

"Help yourself to potatoes, Isobel," said my Aunt.

Appropriate cards for a little girl who confined her dog to a doll's pram and whose middle name was Violet.

"No, thank you," replied Sister. "I don't like them." This was quite true, but a little voice was heard from the other end of the table:

"She doen't eat potatoes 'cos they give her diarrhoea."

"That's the last time you get taken out to dinner!"

One particular weekend, when my Wolverhampton Aunt and Uncle were staying, we had a rather special treat. A Canada Goose had flown into the overhead cables and broken both its wings. I, of course, was unaware of this sad situation until a large roasted bird appeared on the Sunday dinner table. All looked with anxious eyes as Father carved the bird. Suddenly, a small lead shot rolled across the plate. Father looked at Uncle Dick and they both looked at me. Not a word was spoken until Uncle said:

"You've left the point of the knife in that piece, eh, John?" This, I am sure, needs no interpretation. Manna from heaven was this. A real luxury for those days, especially as Canada Geese were protected.

Isobel's secret joy was opera. Father could never understand why she liked to sit up late at night glued to the Crystal Set earphones, listening spellbound to relays from Covent Garden.

One night, she was in the living room, enthralled with *La Bohème*. Even above the sound of the music she could hear the dull thud of Father's footsteps on the wooden stairs. Suddenly, the latch clicked and the door swung open revealing Father in all his glory. He had been at the "poison" again and had put on his short underpants in rather a hurry. Through Isobel's disastrous washing efforts, the legs had stretched to several times their intended width. In his impatience to come downstairs, he had put both legs in the same hole! The only words he uttered were:

"How much longer are you going to sit here, listening to that bloody catawalling?"

By now, I was awake and had jumped out of bed to see what all the rumpus was about. I was just in time to see Father making his way back to bed and taking very short steps. I quietly told him:

"You'd better take off your underpants or else you won't be able to turn over in bed."

"Never you worry about me, my wench. I'm as steady as a rock." And into bed he tumbled.

"Oh," I thought, "So tonight I'm his wench. Usually, I'm the light of his life!"

Soon the house was quiet again, and Isobel could listen to her opera in peace. Highbrow music didn't appeal to Father. He was much happier listening to Elsie Carlisle singing *Home James and Don't Spare the Horses.*

"Right", said Father, one day in 1937, "get your best bib and tucker out. We're going over Cadbury's factory tomorrow."

This announcement came as a bit of a shock.

"You had better take a note to school to explain to the teacher that you will be away tomorrow."

Father was a great believer in doing things the proper way. Playing truant from school just wasn't done. In any case, any child missing from class very soon had the School Inspector breathing down his/her neck. A good explanation would be required. It didn't take him long to pedal round on his bicycle and his shiny brown leggings could be seen a mile away. I think that he was feared rather more than the Headmaster. A jolly good dressing down from him and it would be a long while before you tried staying away again.

Well, off I went to school with my note and the great day dawned.

"For heaven's sake", complained Isobel, "brush your hair and make sure that it's tidy today. You usually look as if the birds have been nesting in it. And mind you wash your ears." Goodness me, I thought, this is meant to be an outing, not a school nit inspection!

We started very early, Father and I, and after numerous bus and tram journeys eventually arrived at Bournville at 11.30am. The first thing I was aware of as we walked from Selly Oak to Bournville was the sweet smell which floated on the wind. Little did I realise that I would much later walk this same way dressed as a student nurse when I was training at the local hospital.

The tour of the factory was really interesting. I was already familiar with some of the products as raw cocoa and finished chocolate was transported by canal boat past my house. It was the first time I had been inside a factory and I found the noise from the machinery quite frightening. I was fascinated by the sight of a huge floor where girls in white hats and overalls sat at long conveyor belts, decorating, sorting and packing chocolates. Imperfect ones were put into fawn-coloured paper bags bearing the words "Cadbury's Waste". I couldn't help but think what a monotonous job this must be. What a boring way to earn a living! Yet some of them had done the work for years. Some, I knew quite well, for they regularly came to the Reservoir for fishing and

How we looked in 1914, Tardebigge School.

brought me treats such as those delicious little bars of Cadbury's Turkish Delight. It was common knowledge that I was especially fond of them.

I was probably much more interested in the factory garden with its displays of flowers. Anyway, I was determined to enjoy the occasion as Father had said:

"Make the most of it. It won't happen again."

At the end of the conducted tour I learned that I was a rather special VIP and that we had only been allowed this visit because Father did so much for the firm. At the end of the momentous day, I was presented with a souvenir tin of selected chocolates, with a

Above: my souvenir chocolate tin.

picture of the Garden Factory printed on the lid. It's getting a little rusty now, half a century later, but nothing would make me give it away!

I would be allowed to spend part of the long summer holidays with my Aunt, Uncle and cousins at Diglis Locks, Worcester. Their name was Watton. Uncle had a large office and was responsible for all the vessels which passed through the Basin, between the canal and the Severn. There was also a very big stable where my cousin Edwin attended to the boat horses. I was allowed to help him.

I could sweep and clean the floor, fill the mangers with hay, put chaff in the horses' feed bags, brush them down and fill the water buckets. If the horses were taken onto the wharf, Edwin would lift me up and I would ride bareback. I loved staying at Diglis as it was a very different life to Tardebigge.

My cousins would take me to the parks and also to the "Pictures". (One just didn't go to the "Cinema" in those days).

One of my best remembered memories of Diglis is the verse which hung in a large frame on the stable wall. I carefully copied it out in pencil on July 2 1933:

The Prayer of A Horse

"To thee, my master, I offer my prayer.
Feed me, water and care for me, and
When the day's work is done, provide
Me with a clean dry bed and stall
Wide enough for me to lie down in comfort.
Talk to me: your voice often means as much to
Me as the reins.
Pet me sometimes, that I may serve you more
Gladly and learn to love you.
Do not jerk the reins, and do not whip me
When going uphill.
Never strike, beat or kick me when I do not
Understand what you mean, but give me a chance
To understand.
Watch me, and if I fail to do your bidding see
If something is wrong with my harness or feet.
Examine my teeth when I do not eat. I may have
An ulcerated tooth and that, you know, is very painful.
Do not tie my head in an unnatural position or take
Away my best defence against flies
And mosquitoes by cutting off my tail.
And finally, oh my master, when my useful
Life is gone, do not turn me out to starve
Or freeze, or sell me to some cruel owner to be
Slowly tortured and starved to death, but do thou,
My master, take my life in the kindest way and
Your God will reward you, here and hereafter.
You may not think me irreverent if I ask this
In the name of Him who was born in a stable."

ANON

What a lovely, sweet smell a stable has: the boat horses' mangers at Diglis were always spotlessly clean and fresh. I loved the smell of the hay and that dusty, sweaty smell that came from the heavy horses as they were brought in to be bedded down for the night, their hooves clip-clopping over the cobblestones at the entrance to the building. They were so glad to rest their weary bodies and settle down for the night. If they were very hot, Edwin would rub them down with straw and I would help. Another reason why I liked staying at Diglis was the tap water, gas light and water closet.

I enjoyed walking up Sidbury to the Co-op and as I grew older, I was allowed to shop there on my own. It was exciting to wander through the town, listening to the newsboys on the Cross shouting:

"Git yer evenin' piper! Read all abart it!"

Some evenings, we walked to the parks or along the river by the Cathedral. For a special treat, we called at the fish and chip shop and I would buy a 1d (0.4p) bag of chips. Lovely they were, all soaked in salt and vinegar!

It was a tremendous thrill to be taken to the pictures. Bessie, the youngest of the girls, always seemed to get landed with me and we would walk along Riverside to Worcester Bridge and through the city to one of the Picture Houses. Usually, there was a long queue

Mr and Mrs Herbert Bate, son Fred and me on the frozen Tardebigge Reservoir.

outside, but sometimes the usherette would come and say: "Two 10d (4p) seats at the front. Half price for children."

Bessie always paid, for she worked at one of the glove factories and therefore was quite "rich". I might even get a 2d (0.8p) ice cream if I was lucky. It was very dark in the Picture House and we would be guided to our seats with the aid of a torch. Dim lights would glow on the walls. All around, people were chattering and virtually every seat in the house was taken. Just as you had settled down and made yourself comfortable, someone generally wanted to leave. So, you gathered up all your belongings took a deep breath, and hoped that they would be able to squeeze past. Suddenly, the lights dipped, the velvet curtains parted and a loud cheer filled the air. Music was heard and out of the floor arose the organ with pretty lights shining all around it.

The organist played popular songs and everyone joined in with the singing. This lasted for about fifteen minutes until the organ sank back out of sight and the audience applauded.

Sometimes, the manager of the house came onto the stage to make an announcement. When he had finished, everyone clapped and cheered again. A long light – almost a searchlight – cast its beam across the heads of the audience and a white square appeared above the stage. Then the whole house was filled with music and a voice would be heard, saying:

"If you are thinking of getting married, buried or Christened, consult — your reliable Taxi Service. We will always get you to the church on time."

Black and white slides were then flashed on the screen, giving the name, address and telephone number of some local firm. The next advertisement might say:

"Are you fat, fair and forty? Do you suffer from cold feet, drooping bosoms, hot flushes? If so, consult your local chemist. You will be a new woman before you are sixty."

Bang! Suddenly, the whole house is plunged into darkness. Everyone turns to look up at the projectionist's box, but the darkness is inky black. The manager arrives on the stage to say that it is just a temporary fault and that if everyone sits still, normal service will be resumed shortly. Ah, music once again. A quick flash and then more darkness. Everyone boos . . . another flash: this one to last a few seconds longer. Then more deafening boos and whistles. A cheeky voice roars throughout the darkness:

"I want me money back!"

A child cries: "I want to go 'ome; don't like it 'ere."

Amid the confusion, another child calls out: "I wants to wee."
Only to be answered by a stern adult:

"Sit down and shut up. You just bin."

"I wet me drawers!"

Any answer is lost in the roar of approval that greets a relit
screen. I feel sure it could be heard by the people across the river
watching a cricket match.

The adverts are small in number and local. Then comes a car-
toon: Popeye, Mickey Mouse, Donald Duck or similarly popular
offerings. Sometimes, the main films are silent, but by the mid-
Thirties "talkies" were all the rage. Shirley Temple was everyone's
idol. Then there were Laurel and Hardy, Charlie Chaplin and
George Formby. Even Father once walked all the way to
Bromsgrove to see Paul Robeson in *Saunders of the River.* There
would be an interval when an usherette appeared with a tray of ice
creams around her neck. Some were wrapped in paper, while
others were in little cardboard tubs, each supplied with a flat
wooden spoon.

Then came the main attraction-The News. One or two people
continued to chatter on, but they did at least respond when asked
to keep quiet. The commentator gabbled so fast and the pictures
flashed on and off so quickly, that I found it almost impossible to
follow any part of it. Had Amy Johnson arrived back in England
before she had even landed in Australia? I was never quite sure
just which way she was heading. And in a horse race, the horses
seemed to complete the course before you could blink your eyes.

After all this, the audience settled down to watch the Big Film.
We cried and sobbed over Lassie, laughed and laughed with the
Keystone Cops and drooled, goggle-eyed at Rudolph Valentino. At
the end, we all stood for the National Anthem and everyone left in
an orderly fashion. If it was daytime, the light outside made me
blink for minutes on end.

Travelling to Worcester and back was a tremendous adventure
as it entailed a very long train journey. It was a good three mile
walk to the railway station where I would sit excitedly on the
platform, waiting for the train to come in. The homeward journey
was always late at night when it was quite dark. Street lights were
very few and far between, but the station waiting room had a good
fire in winter and I could buy a bar of chocolate from a slot
machine for one penny.

I would curl up on the seat in the carriage and listen to the
sound of the wheels as they sang "clickety-clack', while the train

rolled and chugged down the line. In no time at all, I was asleep.

Suddenly, the train would screech to a halt and a voice called out through the darkness: "Bromsgrove Station". Still half asleep, I would hear Father saying:

"Come on, my lassie, we've a long walk home."

The winding lanes to Tardebigge seemed endless.

In 1935, when I was 11 years old, Uncle Will and Aunt Lily from the Top Lock informed my Father that their eldest daughter Nellie was to be married and they would like me to be a bride's maid. I was very excited. What a change it would make to hear people talking about a wedding after so many funerals! But there were no cars waiting at the door for the bride and bride's maids: instead, it was a long trek up the towing path with the hem of my frock tucked into my drawers to prevent it getting splashed with mud. Twenty one members of the Warner family were present for the photograph by the Top Lock.

Nellie Warner's wedding to Bill Bryant. There are 21 Warners in the picture. I am the bridesmaid on the left; Father is left of the groom; Isobel second front the right.

CHAPTER THREE

The Cut

THE Worcester & Birmingham Canal was built at the beginning of the 19th century as a link between the River Severn and Birmingham. It was opened to traffic in 1815. At the head of a great chain of locks, Tardebigge Reservoir occupied part of what had once been Hewell Estate farmland. It was dug out at the same time as the canal was cut and the huge quantity of resulting clay was used to line the canal's bottom, in order to make it watertight. When all the clay had been excavated, the great pit was equipped with paddles, sluice gates, pipes and pumps and was then used to store surplus storm water. These supplies were pumped back to the canal at its summit above Tardebigge Top Lock, by the New Wharf.

The Old Wharf was the first to be built and an inn was later erected on the site – the Navigation. At one period, there was another pub between the two wharves, known as the Squirrel. Additionally, there was the Plymouth Arms which still stands on Tardebigge Tunnel, opposite the New Wharf. Many years ago, the licence for intoxicating liquor was withdrawn from the Plymouth Arms by one of the Earls of Plymouth. When I was a child, it was known as the Plymouth Guest House and a notice outside the front door proclaimed that it was operated by the Temperance Society.

During the last century, the Psalms at the Sunday morning service in Tardebigge church lasted an unusually long time. Lady Harriet Windsor was determined to discover the reason and it appeared that the then vicar enjoyed his pint of ale. While the congregation ploughed its way through the everlasting Psalms, the vicar would have popped over to the Magpie Inn (just 25 yards across the churchyard) for a drink, returning just before the last Psalm had ended. Lady Harriet promptly closed the Magpie and the building was converted into a church school. It was here that generations of village children were taught the three Rs and the bible, with sewing for the girls. Thereafter, any Plymouth Estate land that was sold was done so on the understanding that "No licensed premises or brothels would be allowed".

About 1950, workmen excavating a trench at Tardebigge unearthed a set of metal rails on wooden sleepers. These were the remains of a small railway leading from low ground which had once been a quarry and wending its way in the direction of the church. This track was used to transport stone when the church was built in 1776, and thus was in use long before the canal was cut.

A building known as the Engine House was situated halfway between the reservoir and the Top Lock. Within was the steam-driven beam engine that pumped the water supplies.

There are 58 locks on this stretch of canal. The Top Lock at Tardebigge is at the bottom of Church Hill, with the church spire towering above it. This is the summit lock, deepest of all, with a rise and fall of 14 feet.

My childhood neighbour, George Bate BEM, came from a family who served the canal from 1812 to 1968. 1 am grateful to his family for allowing me the use of his copious notes made about the history of the waterway.

George's great grandfather, Charles Bate, was present at the canal's opening, having started work as a blacksmith in 1812. He had trained in his father's forge in the village of Hanbury, where the Worcester & Birmingham Canal makes a junction with the Droitwich Canals. In 1850, George's grandfather John Bate came into the canal business, acting as an agent between the canal company and the local farmers regarding the collection of farm produce for transport by boat from Stoke Prior Wharf to Birmingham.

George's grandfather, John Bate, lived at the Red Lion at Bradley Green, near Feckenham, Worcestershire. Later, he moved with his family to the Queen's Head on the canal at Stoke pound. Here, he opened a blacksmith's shop to shoe the horses and donkeys towing the working boats up and down the navigation. There was also another canal blacksmith near the Boat and Railway Inn. His name was Stanworth. Young George was born in 1901 and lived with his parents, sister Mildred and four brothers Charlie, Alf, Bill and Fred on the canalside at Whitford Bridge, Stoke Prior. In 1917, the family moved to live in the Reservoir Cottage, Tardebigge.

It was here, in the cottage next door to my home, that I first met the Bates. I spent many happy hours with George's mother and father and although the family were then all grown up, they treated me as if I were their sister. Mrs Bate Senior was like a mother to me. I loved to watch the brothers diving off the lock gates into the pound; sometimes they would even dive into the lock itself. How I envied them! My father would not allow me to swim in the canal: indeed, I was very much older before I learned to swim at all. The nearest I ever got in those days was to dangle my feet over the weir hole on a very hot day.

Sometimes I would walk to Tardebigge New Wharf to gaze at Tommy Insull the blacksmith shoeing the boat horses. As soon as the big bellows were put to work, the embers of the fire would burst into flame. My next move was to call on George Bate, the carpenter, who fashioned the huge lock gates from massive pieces of timber. Oak or Spanish Chestnut from the Hewell Estate was normally used. When the sawmill was built in 1921, using larch trees from the Estate, they were rolled into the canal and towed through the tunnel in rafts.

George's father, Herbert Bate, was a carpenter and joiner on the W & B Canal from 1894–1932. Young George became very interested in canals before he started school and could earn a shilling (5p) on a Saturday morning, rolling oakum for George Farrin. This was a stringy hemp fibre, produced by taking apart old ropes, which was used for caulking the seams of the wooden boats. From the age of 12 until his retirement in 1968, he worked as a canal carpenter, carrying on part time for four years until 1972.

After the death of his parents, he moved with his wife Gladys to Reservoir Cottage from Stoke Prior. Their only son Terry now lives at the Top Lock with his wife and family. He had an amazing memory of much that had happened throughout his life on the canal, and would, I know, have been pleased that some of his stories have been recorded in this book.

During World War II, the Bournville Aqueduct received a direct hit from a bomb, breaking the masonry arch and draining the water from that length of canal. Much damage was caused in the basement of Cadbury's factory. It might have been much worse if stop gates had not been closed at each end of the embankment. George was in the maintenance gang who were ordered to carry out the repairs. He kept a Worcester & Birmingham Canal notebook throughout his life from the age of twelve, and I was able to discover all kinds of fascinating tales within these pages.

Work began on a vertical boat lift at Tardebigge in 1806. Invented by John Woodhouse, progress was slow, but the structure was completed by June 1808. Serious tests started in 1808. A single wooden caisson, 72ft x 8ft wide and 4½ft deep weighed 64 tons when filled with water. This was suspended on eight sets of rods on chains which passed over 12ft diameter cast iron wheels and down to wooden frames containing brickwork forming the counterbalance. The eight wheels were arranged on a common axle, rotated by a low-geared windlass-operated winch. Four wooden guillotine gates stopped off the lengths of canal and the ends of the caisson. When a boat needed to enter or leave the tank, sluices were used to fill with water the gap between the pairs of gates, thus relieving the pressure and allowing the guillotines to be moved up or down.

The lift could be operated by two men and it was claimed possible for a boat to pass through in just 2½ minutes. Its best ever performance was 110 boats in 12 hours. The company's committee requested the famous engineer John Rennie to come and pass his opinion on the device, as it was believed it might not be strong enough to stand the test of time. He agreed with the

Lock gate.

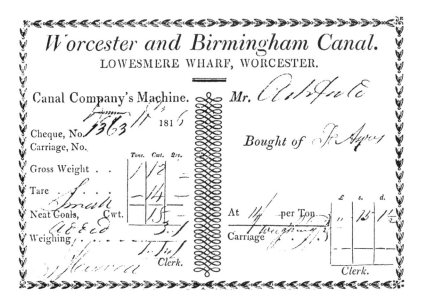

A Worcester & Birmingham Canal toll ticket dated 1816.

majority of the committee, saying that the numerous moving parts would undoubtedly result in heavy maintenance bills.

The lift was dismantled after it was damaged in a cloud burst and the Top Lock built in its present form with the greatest rise and fall of any narrow beam lock in England.

In 1892, two brothers came to Stoke Works to set up a boat building business which flourished for the next half century. Farrin's Dock was owned by George and Joseph Farrin, two men who had learned the craft of building flat bottomed and keel boats alongside the Grand Junction Canal at Stowe Hill, near Weedon, Northamptonshire. Their yard was at the eastern end of the Stoke Salt Works and was mainly employed in building and repairing the boats that carried John Corbett's salt around the country.

John Corbett was the son of a canal boat owner but was not interested in developing his own carrying business. Salt production took all his time and he made it pay. Boat building and repairing was left to the Farrin Brothers. They mended craft in the summer and built new ones in the winter, providing employment for thirteen men, including their nephew, Thomas Farrin of Bromsgrove, Fred Lyne, Bob Lewis and Tommy Hodges who was the last Tardebigge boat builder and a friend of canal author Tom

Rolt. These highly skilled craftsmen worked with saw, adze and plane from dawn until dusk. They shaped the curved bows of the narrow boats and carried the great side planks sizzling hot out of the steam box in order to create the graceful curves of bow and stern.

They painted the castles and roses which gave a fairy-tale appearance to cabins and water cans. Even the "guzunder" (which "guz under the bed") had bunches of roses on it.

The first motor-driven boat to be launched in this dock was the *Enterprise*, made for T & M Dixon of Tardebigge to carry their milk and poultry into Birmingham. Years later *Enterprise* would pay a visit for a "wash and brush-up" from Tom Farrins' hands. Another regular visitor was Sabrina, a dainty little steamer used on official company inspections of the waterway. One more regular caller was the tug *Harriet*, older than *Sabrina*. Before World War *1*, *Sabrina* was renamed *Little Sabrina* and remained in steam until 1917. Her 1890-built steam engine was removed and a petrol unit put in its place, but she was little used after 1919. For nine years the original steam engine lay in silt at the bottom of the

Top lock Diglis Basin, Worcester and Townsends flour mill.

canal. It was later rescued, restored and can be seen in the Waterways Museum at Stoke Bruerne, Northamptonshire.

The lore and traditions of the boat people are fascinating. I would recognise a boatman by the leather straps around his trouser legs, below the knees, while some of the men tied their trouser legs with string. Long socks were not available and in any case would have been too costly. His normal friendly greeting consisted of the two words: "How do?" Although their 7ft x 10ft cabin living quarters were very confined, all the everyday essentials were close to hand. There was clearly a (small) place for everything and everything in its place. There is still much for the sightseer to discover of this way of life in the extensive system of Midlands waterways: old gas lamps and cast iron bridges, caves cut from the sandstone to serve as stabling for the horses, old pump houses, paddles and signboards.

Some of the boat people were ardent Methodists and Salvationists. Sunday evening services would be held on a boat where three or four families had moored up together. To the strains of an accordian, melodeon, Jew's harp or mouth organ they would put every possible ounce of feeling into the well known hymns. The eldest male in the gathering would say a prayer and after the "meeting", everyone would make for the nearest pub. They didn't have far to go: there was always one just around the corner.

Then the fun began. A friendly scrap soon produced black eyes, split lips and bleeding noses. It took only a short time for them to turn their attention from bibles to brew and from prayers to pubs.

When a couple decided to be wed, the parents decorated the new floating love nest with crêpe paper, bunting, flowers and ribbons. They would be married in the church nearest to where the boat was tied. The bridegroom would carry his bride from the church to the boat, unless, of course, she was a fairly hefty wench. And then, away they would float in their gondola . . . Wherever a boat was moored, the vicar of that parish would be called on to baptise a baby.

Men's wages were paid every other Friday. The money was brought from the Gas Street office in Birmingham by the wages clerk who travelled out by rail. On arrival at Barnt Green Station, he would be met by the lengthman from Bittell Reservoir and brought to Tardebigge in the Company's car, a 1913 Ford Seven.

A trade union was introduced to the maintenance staff of the canal in 1919: this was the Dock, Wharf & Riverside General

Workers' Union, later to be amalgamated with the T & GWU. This was one time when my Father was very pleased he was not a maintenance worker.

If a boatman died and he was away from his home town or village, he would be brought back in his coffin, slung from the beams of his boat which would be drawn back to the home depot or port by his relations or workmates. All other boats would give way to a vessel that was carrying its skipper on his last journey. Although all manner of dangerous fuels and acids were carried on the canal, accidents were few and far between and seldom did you hear of the loss of life through negligence.

There are five tunnels between Birmingham and Worcester. Edgbaston, just a short one at 105 yards. Then West Hill (King's Norton or Wast Hill), 2,726 yards with no towpath; Shortwood, at 613 yards; Tardebigge, at 580 yards and finally the 230 yard Dunhampstead below the foot of the "Thirties" in the 5 mile pound from Astwood to Offerton.

In 1876, three tugs came from Gloucester District to haul horse boats through the tunnels. They were the *Birmingham, Worcester*

The Engine House.

and *Gloucester.* The crew were all young unmarried men and they lodged either at Tardebigge or King's Norton. Among them were Walter Harries, William Hawkins, the brothers Fred and Issac Bolton, Frank Rowles and William Veale. Some of them lived in a large wooden shed on the New Wharf. Although this was only temporary accommodation used while houses were being built for them, the site is known to this day as Tug Row.

The tugs were a great asset compared with the dangerous job of "legging" boats through the tunnels. But it soon became clear that three tugs were not sufficient and another steam tug, *Stoke* was built at Stoke Prior maintenance depot. This allowed for two tugs working and two in reserve. Five oil-engined tugs, built by the Thames & Severn Canal yard of Abdela & Mitchell went into service in 1908–9: *Birmingham, Worcester, Stoke, Droitwich* and *Sharpness.* Three have lasted to the present, *Worcester* being an exhibit at the Boat Museum, Ellesmere Port, while *Birmingham* and *Sharpness* are in private hands as a workboat and pleasure cruiser respectively. *Sharpness'* engine would start up on petrol and then turn over to paraffin oil. If she had a heavy tow through

Winding gear on double gates on locks.

West Hill, her exhaust would belch out great clouds of fumes and the crew would be over come with "sleepy sickness". To overcome the problem, a fan driven by a gas engine was installed on the middle air shaft and this drew out the fumes. The gas engine was operated by a Mr J Howard, who lived at Hopwood.

In 1910, the maintenance department was transferred from Stoke Prior to Tardebigge. Frank Rowles took on the post of manager and had a house built for him in 1913, almost opposite the Plymouth Inn. A toll cottage had once stood on this site, serving the road that was closed when the canal was built.

At this period, commercial trade for the canal came from Avonmouth Docks, Sharpness, Gloucester and Worcester and in spite of the competition from railways remained very steady until after World War I.

Over the years, the same surnames were to be found among the boat people. Family traditions were handed down from one generation to the next. Names such as Birch, Mans, Tonks, Parrot, Manley, Brown, Crease, Spiers, Footman and Stokes were all well known to me. But many of these names vanished with the Second World War when the young men served on Inland Waterway Transport in France. Some of the lucky ones acquired army surplus lorries and this increased a decline in canal traffic. Gradually, more and more pleasure boats would be seen.

In 1927, the tug Birmingham sank at the Birmingham end of the West Hill Tunnel. This accident resulted from her being stranded partly on the bank when high water levels followed a torrential thunder storm. As the water receded, she toppled over onto her side. It cost a gang of men much sweat to lift and refloat her once more.

The tug crew worked to a tight schedule, working on a two-shift arrangement in Summer from 4.00am to 8.00pm. As many as fourteen boats were towed through the tunnels every two hours. Only one accident was recorded during the 56 years that George Bate worked on the Worcester & Birmingham Canal. This was in 1930, when dredger man John Wolfindale had the end of his thumb scrubbed off on the side of the West Hill Tunnel wall. He pushed the boat's tiller too far over . . .

I was taken through Tardebigge Tunnel at a very early age, but I remember that it was not a very unusual experience, for I was already used to travelling through train tunnels.

In the early days of the canal, the toll clerks acted as agents in getting trade for the local farmers. These clerks had at their disposal a horse that they could ride down the towpath to contact farmers or Number One (owner/operator) boatmen. They would also carry messages to lock keepers, work gangs and lengthsmen. This was before the telephone was installed. Up to 1940, all the waterway's telephones were private, for use on canal business only. This mainly consisted of connecting lock keepers with the nearest wharf. In those days, the telephone wires were fixed along the tunnel walls. A gang of men were one day repairing an insulator when suddenly one of them fell backwards across the boat cabin. His mates thought he must have fainted, so they moved the boat out into the open as quickly as possible. Only then did they realise that a violent thunder storm was taking place overhead and that their colleague had received an electric shock.

There have been many tales of ghosts in the tunnels. Anyone boating through is confronted by a dense patch of mist before the phantom appears. In Finstall churchyard (close to where I would watch Big Bertha puffing up the railway's Lickey Incline) lies the body of Richard Jones, canal worker, who died at the age of 46

Tardebigge Tunnel, 1985.

years. His headstone was erected by his fellow workmates and some of the tools used by Jones during his years of employment with the Worcester & Birmingham Canal Company are shown on the badly weathered stone. Could it be this man's ghost that haunts the tunnel? Correspondence in the *Bromsgrove Advertiser & Messenger* in February 1984 suggests otherwise. Jones lived at Bitford Lock, Claines Parish, Worcester. (Curiously my Father once lived there also). On the dark night of April 30 1840, Richard Jones emerged from the Crown Inn, jar of ale in hand, and decided to get some sleep in the centre of the Droitwich Road, where he was duly run over by the Bristol-Birmingham Mail. Humphries, the coachman, was fully acquitted by the inquest jury. Somehow, it seems rather an ignominious way to die: especially when you have such a fine and elaborate tombstone!

But canal ghosts have been seen and are fully believed in. Many years ago, a young lad working a boat with his father had heard tell of the ghost in Tardebigge Tunnel. When they arrived at Tardebigge, the boatman told his young son to walk the horse over

Richard Jones' tombstone in Finstall churchyard, with a representation of some of the tools he used in his work for the Canal Company.

the top, across the Shaws, while the tug pulled the boat through. Legend tells that the ghost waits by the big gate which leads onto the road between the Shaws and the Old Wharf. A great argument blew up between father and son. The father told the lad not to be a baby and to get on with the job.

"But", replied the boy, "It's six o'clock in the morning and it's pitch dark."

"Git that 'oss across them Shaws and stop thee frettin'. Tain't no such thing as ghosts."

This particular boat was empty, so there was no need for her to be steered behind the tug. When the boy had set off, his father thought that maybe he had been a bit hard on the kid and set off after him. Knowing a short cut, he arrived at the gate well before his son and was prepared for a long wait.

So, horse and boy plodded quietly across the Shaws, the lad whispering to the horse about how mean his father was, while all the time clinging to the reins so tightly that the leather cut into the palms of his hands. Meanwhile, the mist grew thicker and thicker.

"Woah up a bit", said the lad. "I want to keep as close to you as I can; we're nearly at the gate."

Raising his head slightly, he saw through the fog the outline of a figure standing at the gate. The poor lad was so terrified that he fainted on the spot.

There were eighty pairs of donkeys used by the Canal Company for towing on the Worcester & Birmingham and the Staffordshire & Worcestershire Canals. They worked in pairs, side by side and soon got used to working in each other's company, like real pals. But heaven help you if you had a pair that didn't know one another and had never worked together. Often, it was possible to take a small donkey through a "clap" gate across the towpath, but there would be problems when the one went through and the other refused. Further difficulties arose where the path was very narrow. This would happen in Bittell Cutting, so they tried working them in single file. But this turned out to be a very slow process, as the lead donkey kept turning around to see if his mate was following! However, they were both good and useful if and when you had a well-matched pair.

The donkeys knew every part of the canalside and just where to stop at the locks. Although they didn't know when to start, they invariably knew when to stop. They also knew the whereabouts of every stable and that as soon as they left Tardebigge there would be a little girl waiting at Lock 53 to give them some carrots. I love them still.

The Company also owned two donkeys that would work on their own, one at Stoke Prior and the other at Worcester. A small cart was made specially for them to take horse corn to different parts of the canal in the locality.

During World War 1, Tardebigge Village Hall was turned into a hospital for wounded soldiers. Numerous herbs were grown in the ground at the back: poppies for opium, foxgloves for digitalis, comfrey, parsley, deadly nightshade and many more. The soldiers, who were able, enjoyed a walk to the New Wharf, where they found peace and tranquility, thousands of miles from the muddy hell of the trenches and the Battle of the Somme. They liked to go into the carpenter's shop and talk to Herbert Bate, George's father, watching him shape a lock gate, or fitting a new plank in a boat.

World War I soldiers during their convalescence, seen outside Tardebigge Village Hall.

They had endless tales to tell and Herbert Bate was a good listener, as he had served for nine years in Egypt with the Royal Engineers.

George was most interested in their experiences and tales of what had happened in France. Most of all, they liked to ride on the steam tugs or travel with George on a boat behind the tug. Often, there were eight or ten young men setting out on a great adventure through Tardebigge and Shortwood Tunnels. Once they had reached the inky blackness at the tunnel centre, they would give

Worcester – Birmingham tunnel tug Worcester, seen at Tardebigge, probably early 1930s. John Colledge and Percy Hawkins on board. She is now exhibited at the Boat Museum, Ellesmere Port.

vent to their feelings. Many of them had had a truly dreadful time. Canalside workmen each end of the tunnel would put down their tools and stand like statues as the sound of men singing drifted out of the dark hole. They sang just for the pure joy of it; for the relief at being away from the Front. Their singing mingled with the vibration of the engine and the gurgle of water from the propellor. One of their favourite songs was:

"Where are the boys of the village tonight?
Where are the lads we knew?
In Piccadilly or Leicester Square,
No, not there, no not there.
Taking a trip on the Continent
With their rifles and bayonets bright.
Going across the water to see the Kaiser's daughter.
That's where they are tonight."

George was very fond of this song. I remember that my father sang it too in the Halfway House. There was another ditty that the men liked, but I'm not going to repeat it here. It was about "telling the Sergeant Major what to do with his passes . . ."

In the winter of 1915–16, two soldiers of the South Staffordshire Regiment were sent to dismantle and break up the beam engine and boiler from the Engine House off the London Road. It had not been in regular use for many years, but had been kept in good order and turned over periodically. The last recorded date of use was January 1914, just as a maintenance run. This magnificent engine was secondhand when installed in 1820. What a shame that it was not allowed to be preserved as a museum piece.

In 1918, German prisoners of war were billeted at the Dusthouse Farm, recently bought by T & M Dixon from the Taylor family. They were put to work in the fields between the London Lane and the Grimley Lane, tearing up hedgerows to make one big field out of four or five small ones. They would come to Reservoir Cottage during the day for drinking water and would talk to Mr and Mrs Bate about their homes and families. They would unload boats filled with manure from Birmingham and spread it on the land which they had cleared. If it was a warm day, they would swim in the canal during their lunch break . . . in the nude.

At the end of World War I, the canal was exceptionally busy. Among the cargoes carried were raisins, currants, sultanas, candied peel and other dried fruits, all packed in boxes as part of the Christmas trade. Then there was candle fat and rubber, glass jars and bottles, even gunpowder, packed in special containers. All types of building materials, imports of coffee, a zinc-based metal known as "spelter", aluminium, iron, steel, many types of crude oil, wheat, corn, maize, oats, barley and a species of wheat called "spelt" whose grains produce a very fine flour.

As many as 75 boats in one day, mostly loaded, have been recorded between Tardebigge and Stoke Prior. Empty boats coming down the locks would stop at Stoke to load large blocks of salt to take on to Gloucester. Here, they were reloaded into oceangoing vessels bound for Australia. The Severn & Canal Carrying Company owned the largest fleet of boats, around 130 of them, all horse-drawn and named after towns and villages along the waterways. Other big fleets, with about 50 boats in each, belonged to Jacob Rice Ltd, James Waldron of Gloucester, James Stuart of Stroud, and Chadburn, Son & Taylor of Gloucester.

By 1901, there were about 86 men employed on the Company's maintenance staff as well as toll clerks, office workers and weighing machine clerks, At Gas Street, Birmingham, there were

Repairing the locks, 1930.

three gangs of brick layers, six men to a gang; four carpenters making two gangs and these carpenters would be assigned to work with a gang of labourers numbering anything up to a dozen men, depending on the size of the job in hand. There were eleven lock keepers. Two lock keepers and one toll clerk employed on the Droitwich Canal (also operated by the Sharpness New Docks & Gloucester & Birmingham Navigation Company) would sometimes be called on to make up working strength on the Worcester & Birmingham.

Repair stoppages took place every Monday during the summer in the Stoke Prior area. Bigger jobs, requiring weeklong stoppages were scheduled for the Easter, Whitsun and August Bank Holidays. The men worked from first light until dusk, refitting lock gates and paddles or perhaps rebricking a chamber wall. It was the lock keeper's responsibility to stack a suitable supply of turf by the towing path in readiness for the stoppage. This turf would be placed on the flat side of wooden beams known as "scour planks". Each measured about 12ft x 2ins x 11ins. The water would be drained from the pound and the plank placed edgeways on the "scour" (bottom of the canal). Metal bars called "staunch bars" would be driven into the canal bed to keep the plank on its edge. Turf was then placed on and along the side of the plank that would take the pressure of the water. When finished, there would be nine to twelve planks on different parts of the "scour", placed so that the men could stand on them and so keep out of the water that had to be scooped from the almost empty lock chamber.

Wooden hand scoops were used to pour all surplus water from the lock to the other side of the staunch plank. Sometimes it would take a dozen men, scooping away in unison, 1½ hours to lower the water sufficiently for three men to stand on the clap sills to scoop water over them to the gang scooping water over the staunch planks. This arduous method continued to be used until the introduction of mobile motor pumps.

Elsewhere, steam or manual pumps of timber and iron were lowered into the lock by the stop planks and a stage fixed for the men to work from. When the pump was primed, up to six men would take the handle and heave away for half an hour, when they would be relieved by another six. By this method, it took two hours to drain a lock. All the time, the men could be heard singing songs, ditties and sea shanties, seemingly happy about their work.

Later, another method was tried, using a steam powered centrifugal pump, driven by belt and pulley. Two of these were in use with heavy iron pipes that had to be bolted together at the flanges. The first petrol pump used an Aster motor: this was hung over the end of a 45ft narrow boat and was first tried out by a carpenters' gang at Easter 1916.

The next pumping improvement was a 4 inch model mounted on a chassis with iron wheels and driven by an engine removed from the De Dion Bouton motor car belonging to Tardebigge schoolmaster, Mr Dilks. This was brought into service for many years at all locks that had long pounds below.

In 1936, a 12 year old boy named Leslie Williams came to live with his parents near the waterway at Alvechurch. He had long been fascinated by the canal, and now he was living only 500 yards from it, watching the boats go by and constantly asking questions. Like me, he could beg a ride on a boat, know what cargo it carried, lead the horse along the towpath and work the gates and paddles. When he was fourteen, he started to spend every Saturday helping at the locks. At 6.00 am, it was all aboard the *Medway*, a Droitwich Salt Works boat. Together with Wilf Colledge, Danny Merrell and another young friend, they would set out from Alvechurch to be towed through Shortwood and Tardebigge Tunnels to the New Wharf. Often, Leslie would walk the horse along the lanes over the tunnels. They then worked through the locks, sometimes calling at the Halfway House for a glass of pop.

They would arrive at Stoke Works about 1.00pm, where the task of loading the boat with huge blocks of salt began. Each was about 2ft 6ins long and weighed 28 pounds. Fully laden, the boat could carry about 11 tons. All loading and unloading was done by hand. And after the day's exertions, they would either walk home along the canal or hitch a ride aboard a craft travelling back up to Tardebigge. For the weekly trip they were paid a mere 6d each (2½p). Destination for the loaded salt boats was Gas Street Basin, Birmingham. Here, the blocks would be cut up and sold to shops and factories. Other customers were farmers who used the salt for home cured bacon.

Most of the normal stopping places on the salt run had a pub nearby, for boating was a thirsty job for man and horse. You can still see the weather-worn stone or wooden bollards where the boats tied up. At Withybed Green, there is an old "split" bridge, always known to the boat people as 'Ave Up Bridge (heave up).

The last salt boat from Stoke Works was the *Joan*. Charlie Ballinger owned the *Edna Grace*, while another of his boats, originally *Thomas*, was renamed *Energy*. The Severners (boats of the Severn & Canal Carrying Company) were referred to as "towrags", a nickname that came about from the process known as "bow-hauling". Bow-hauliers were a band of men, generally ill-paid casual labourers, who towed the boats from the bank, digging the toes of their boots into the lockside cobblestones. In time, their boots and socks also would become worn and ragged: hence the name "towrags".

Fellows, Morton & Clayton was one of the largest carriers in the Birmingham area. The boats were popularly known as "Joshers" after a Victorian director of the Company, Joshua Fellows. While more than two dozen of their craft had once been steam-powered, in my day their semi-diesel engines were fuelled by crude oil at 6d (2½p) a gallon. Local cargoes carried included copper, tea, sugar, coal, matches, timber, cocoa and chocolate crumb (a form of semiprocessed chocolate).

Other boats I remember were the *Stoke, Hanbury, Broms-grove, Worcester and Gloucester;* and craft carrying hay, tar, oil, and flour from Townsend's Mill at Worcester, England's Glory matches from Gloucester and coal from Cannock Chase.

There were also the Number One (owner/operator) boatmen. The Colledge family of New Wharf, Tardebigge were also boaters. Tom Colledge helped his father with the coal boat, sometimes assisted by his brother Frank. As a young lad, Tom was intrigued by the rules of the cut: horse boats must keep to the towpath side; loaded boats to keep to the deep water; when passing, keep to the right; mooring lines not to be stretched across the towpath; and all cyclists must have a towpath permit, otherwise they would soon have a lock keeper after them. All sensible regulations, designed to ensure the smooth working of the canal.

Most of the boat people lived in a world of castles and roses, with a range of designs painted on the boats, tillers and water cans. The type of castle depicted on the cabin doors depended on the boatyard which carried out the work. Sometimes there were touches of Windsor or Warwick; more often it would be a fantastic Neuschwanstein pattern or one seemingly inspired by the fairy tale castles of Eastern Europe. Inside the cabin there might be a tray to match, a copy of the old Brummagem tin ware. I was once told by a boatman's wife that the roses were a sign of remembrance and affection. They would certainly be overjoyed if we gave them a bunch of roses from our garden.

The women were jolly, plump and had rosy cheeks. They wore fairly long, full-skirted dresses with brightly coloured pinafores topped by a warm coat and headscarf in the cold weather. You would never see a boatman's wife wearing trousers. The children were as well dressed as you would expect for this time and never seemed hungry, cold or ill-treated. These boat people were friendly and dependable and thought the world of their mules and horses. They would rather be penniless than give up their animals.

I would stand on the towpath outside our house and gaze longingly at a boat rising in the lock. Sometimes the boatman's wife would shout:

"Come on then, young Pat! Jump on and 'ave a ride to the next lock."

I needed no further encouragement. All aboard: that was me! I might hold the tiller or just sit on the cabin top by the brightly painted water cans. If it was cold, I sat in the cabin by the warm stove. The boat children would call out:

"Got any apples, Mr Warner?"

And Father would fill their caps and pockets with rosy apples and pears. If the weather was rough, a padlock would be attached to the paddles to stop the lock being used and to thus prevent accidents on dark and stormy nights. The boat would then be tied up in the pound until the next morning and we would find ourselves with new neighbours for a short while.

Most of the narrow boats were both pretty and very clean with bright paintwork. Inside the tiny cabin, coloured blankets covered the bed and often the sweet smell of raw chocolate (known as "crumb") would drift through from the hold. The cabin brasswork shone like gold and the ribbon plates tinkled with a music of their own as the boat rocked on the water.

At the back of the rudder was a stern fender of plaited rope, while some of the boats hung a horse's tail from the "Ram's Head" (rudder). This tradition, resulted, it is said, from a boatman losing a favourite animal and wishing to be reminded of his faithful friend's working days and loyalty.

One boat that held a great fascination for me was the dredger, used for scooping mud off the bed of the canal. The gang consisted of four men: Tom Wolfindale and his son John, Tom Spiers and Harry Waldron. It would be towed by two men wearing a large leather sling around their shoulders. This was attached to a rope fixed to the boat. Equally, the dredging equipment was worked manually: a large, spoon-like shovel suspended from a small crane. Each time the spoon was dipped into the water it would be wound up containing half a hundredweight of mud or "spoil". This

Entering lock 56.

Entering lock 57.

was tipped into the mud boat moored alongside and reserved for this purpose only.

There was an art in dredging. If the spoon was dipped too deep it would damage the puddled clay lining of the canal and cause leaks.

Boat people and other canal workers were noted for their clothes: hobnail boots or wooden clogs, rough hard-wearing trousers held up with a wide, leather belt, a shirt with a collar band, a woollen or serge waistcoat, a jacket and a cap. Father had a permanent "hump" in his jacket, for he carried his windlass (lock handle) on his shoulder. In later years he might also keep it in his belt. He always said of the canal:

"I have lived here all my life and I'll die here. The only way I'll leave this cottage will be in a wooden box!"

Equally, times were very hard on occasion. During World War 1, it was a case of the survival of the fittest. With coal selling at ten shillings (50p) per cwt, it was not unknown for lads to creep aboard a coal boat moored for the night and push a little of the cargo into the cut. When the boat had moved on next day, they

Round Pound bridge at the foot of the Tardebigge Reservoir lock 56.

would dive in and retrieve their prize. And the hunt for spilled coal would begin in earnest if part of the canal should be drained for maintenance.

It was a very rare happening to be bothered or worried about a suspicious character lurking about the cut. Isobel was sometimes dubious about some of Father's tales, related after his visits to the Halfway House. Nevertheless, we were keen to listen to any story he might wish to relate:

"By Jove, there was a rum-looking cus in the snug tonight", he once began, as he was sitting down to put on his slippers. Just at that very moment who should walk past the house but the "rumlooking cus"! He was gazing into the empty lock.

"Do you think he's going to jump in?" I asked excitedly. "I've never seen a body floating in the cut!"

"And you're not likely to see one on this night of Our Lord" replied Father, sharply. "Off to bed, and don't stare through the window. It's very rude."

As I climbed the stairs I thought it wouldn't matter now if I peeped round the curtains. As the man turned away from the edge of the lock I saw that he was very tall, lean and gaunt. He wore a battered old trilby and a long, faded and shabby raincoat. The bottoms of his trousers were ragged and his shoes were badly worn. He had a long black beard. I thought that it was a good thing that it was Summertime and the nights were light. I might have missed him if it had been winter. But I need not have worried, as, on my way home from school next day, skipping down the towpath I had just come under the London Road bridge when who should I see lying fast asleep on the bank but the "rum-looking cus" of the night before. He must have been sound asleep because he had not stirred when I sang and shouted to hear the echo under the bridge.

I tiptoed past, very cautiously, holding my breath until I was at a safe distance. I then stood still and gazed at the man. Suddenly I realised:

"Oh, I know who it is! It's Jesus Christ. They said in church today that the Lord will come and not be slow!" I ran down the canal as fast as my legs would carry me.

Just who this mysterious stranger, the "rum cus", was I never learned. He would spend the night in the fishermen's hut on the reservoir bank. Perhaps he was a spy, for there was now frequent talk of war. Maybe he was just a loner. Father gave him some bread and dripping and a mug of tea, but we never got him to talk.

The locals called him Lazarus and concluded that he belonged to a religious sect.

One night he sat in the Halfway House. The men were chatting and as usual were in a jolly mood. Some of them were listening to Father's rendering of:

"In these old lavender trousers
I've jumped and skipped and skated.
Drunk old ale, drunk champagne
Been up a pole and down a drain.
And twice been vaccinated."

The second verse was funnier and told how a couple had gone to the railway station but couldn't afford to buy a ticket for their son. So they had hidden him inside the old man's lavender trousers. When the ticket collector came round, Sammy had

"Poked his nose through a hole he had found
In those old lavender trousers."

But even all the laughter and applause that followed didn't alter the vacant expression on the face of the "rum cus". He disappeared out of our lives as silently as he had come in.

In the Autumn of 1941 Uncle Will from the Top Lock spoke to Father on the telephone, asking him if he knew anything about the strange houseboat that was now moored at the New Wharf.

"No," said Father. "But don't you forget, our Will. There's a war on and everything is either hush hush or top secret."

Nothing could be done that night, what with the blackout, the searchlights darting across the sky, the distant drone of aeroplanes and the wail of the sirens. Father thought we all had enough to cope with and if the man on the houseboat was a "bloody Gerry" he wouldn't be able to do much damage tonight.

"Better find out who this mystery man is, though," said Father. "You never know: he *might* be a German spy. Maybe the Enemy intended to use the canal for the invasion they have planned. They might be going to drop rubber dinghies out of the sky into the cut! The next thing we shall see is a regiment of jackboots marching down the towpath."

The name of the boat turned out to be *Cressy* and it was home to L T C Rolt and his wife Angela. She was moored at Tardebigge through the war years and to say that Tom Rolt was viewed with suspicion would be putting it mildly.

"What's he doing here?" said one of our neighbours. "Why isn't he away fighting for his country? After all, he's a fairly young man.

"Where does he go?" asked another. "He's away all day and doesn't come back until late at night. What does his wife do, anyway? Don't see much of her, do we?"

"Well, I don't care who the devil he is," remarked Father. "I'm

Outside lock 53 (our house lock) St Johns Ambulance nurse, 1939.

not having him snooping around here asking a lot of questions. I've lived and worked on the canals all my life and I don't intend to be cross-examined."

In fact, Tom Rolt turned out to be anything but a threat to the canals. His wartime service was with the Ministry of Supply, using his training as an engineer. He enjoyed a successful career as a writer with a number of fine books on waterways, among them the classic *Narrow Boat*. This tells of his voyages in *Cressy* shortly before the start of World War 11. *Narrow Boat* was largely instrumental in the formation of the Inland Waterways Association by Tom Rolt, Robert Aickman and Charles Hadfield in 1946. And, but for the IWA, most people agree what few of Britain's canals would now be open to traffic. Something of the Rolts' time at Tardebigge is recounted in Ian Mackersey's *Tom Rolt and the Cressy Years* (M and M Baldwin 1985).

1 saw very little of the Rolts, for he worked long hours and his wife Angela was in the Womens' Land Army. But he always seemed to be the subject of local tittle tattle. John Colledge warned Tom that *Cressy* was "as rotten as a pear" and that she should go into drydock to be checked by the boat builder, Tommy Hodges. But Tom was not happy at this idea and claimed she would be all right without new planking or caulking. Within a few days *Cressy* had started to fill with water and all hands were required to prevent her sinking. She lasted until 1951, when Tom sold her and was finally broken up about 1953, a sad end for such a famous boat that was responsible for much of what we now take for granted on our canals. She had been converted from a freight craft in 1929 – one of the earliest narrow boat conversions.

On the towing path near the "clap" gate where *Cressy* was moored throughout the War, now stands a brick pillar bearing a cast bronze plaque with the following words:

"On this spot in 1946 on board *Cressy*, Tom and Angela Rolt first met Robert Aickman and decided to found the Inland Waterways Association. Erected 1981 by the Worcester & Birmingham Canal Society."

CHAPTER FOUR

Christmas Memories

THE Winter of 1928, it just snowed and snowed. We didn't see the milkman or the postman for a number of weeks. Somehow, this seemed fairly normal in those days and we were always well prepared.

The snow would pile up along the towing path, two or three feet high – sometimes higher. And it was cold. So cold at night that it would freeze the contents of the chamber pot under the bed! I would keep warm with a hot brick wrapped in a piece of flannel. But what a pretty sight was all that snow! Clean, white snow, not dirty, slushy stuff. The sun shining and long icicles hanging from the lock gates. If you looked across the Reservoir from the back bedroom window, you might catch a glimpse of some wild creature which had dared venture out. You might even see a red squirrel, sitting in one of the trees, holding a hazel nut between his front paws.

I knew that if the weather didn't improve, we would be unable to visit my Aunt and Uncle for Christmas. They lived, I thought, on the other side of the world, but it was only Wolverhampton. All that long distance was a great adventure for me. It began with a two-mile walk to the bus stop at Tardebigge. The fare from there to Bromsgrove was 5d (2p). We would then travel to Stourbridge – another shilling (5p) – and from there to the LMS station at Wolverhampton – one more shilling. This would take most of a day. On reaching journey's end, the Wolverhampton snow was all wet and dirty, not like the nice clean snow I was used to.

Most of Christmas Eve was passed in taking trams to visit the shops. What a good thing I liked buses and trams, because not all the dolls and sweets in England would have persuaded me to get into a car. I was terrified of motor cars! The large stores in town stayed open until 8.00 o'clock at night and I would be able to buy all my Christmas presents with the 2s 6d (12½p) I had saved.

We would return to my Aunt's house for supper and go to the midnight service at the huge church in nearby Cannock. There would be a big choir, a lovely crib and (as I then described it) the man with the flat hat would swing the innocents around! The smell of the incense would stay in my nostrils for days. After we left church, my

Aunt and Uncle would curse and argue all the way home.

Here, at my Aunt's, I would sleep in a folding chair. I lay awake for hours, waiting for Father Christmas to come down the chimney. Somehow, I always missed him. I had the same presents in my stocking each year: a large coloured play ball, a sugar pig, an orange and one bright new shining penny.

Christmas in Wolverhampton meant more to me than anything else in the world. For once, there would be water from the tap by the sink; gas light in the kitchen to show me the way across the yard to the WC outside; a gas stove in the kitchen on which to boil the kettle . . . all this was achieved at the turn of a switch. The mantle in the light globe made a funny hissing sound, quite warm and homely. So different to the lamplight at Tardebigge. A gas light glowed in the street just outside the house and friendly noises could be heard from the shunting yard at the nearby railway station.

Aunt Polly had no children and was very house proud. Everything clean and bright, scrubbed and polished, a place for everything and everything in its place. A cheerful coal fire threw out ample heat from a black-leaded grate that shone like glass. So shiny that I could see the reflections of my red cheeks. The only time when Aunt Polly wasn't working was when she was eating, sleeping, praying or playing cards.

There were always nice things to eat with little luxuries like sago pudding. On Christmas morning it was cold boiled ham for breakfast. Uncle worked for the Railway and was "rich"! Afterwards, we dressed in our Sunday Best to attend the Christmas Morning service. But first, always on a Christmas Morning, without fail, my Aunt would scrub the back yard. Down she went on her hands and knees and scrubbed and scrubbed. Meanwhile, my "rich" Uncle became madder and madder, shouting and blaspheming and then hoping that the Good Lord would forgive him.

If we were lucky, we might get our Christmas dinner about 3.00pm. I just couldn't wait for dinner to be cleared away because I knew that afterwards the grown-ups would play cards so they wouldn't need me around. That could only mean one thing:

"Put little Pat into the parlour. There's a nice fire. She can amuse herself."

A lovely fire cast its shadows on the parlour ceiling. It was the only day of the year that this room was open to the public apart from weddings and funerals. The "holy of holies" shone brighter than the Eastern Star! Cards finished, my Uncle could settle down for the great moment he had been waiting for: a sing song around the piano. The walls of 30, Smestow Street, just off the Cannock Road, would ring with the rendering of fine old Victorian Carols. My favourite was *The Mistletoe Bough* by Thomas Haynes Bayly.

"The mistletoe hung in the castle hall.
The holly branch shone on the old oak wall.
The Baron's retainers were blithe and gay
While keeping their Christmas holiday.
The Baron beheld with a fatherly pride
His beautiful child, young Lovell's bride.
She, with her bright eyes, seemed to be
The star of that goodly company.
Oh, the mistletoe bough,
Oh, the misteltoe bough."

Uncle Dick was a good pianist and that never-to-be-forgotten carol made a perfect Christmas. We went home the day after Boxing Day.

I didn't have a Christmas tree, either at home or at my Aunt's. A holly bush would be hung from a large hook in the ceiling at home, provided that the home-cured bacon had first been removed. This top, taken from a holly tree, was a pretty sight, a bow of tinsel, a pink sugar pig and a white sugar mouse being the only decorations. But if filled the house with the spirit and magic of Christmas. I knew that the little pig, with his friend the mouse, would afterwards be returned to their paper wrappings for next Christmas . . . and the next . . . and the next. Eventually, they were so old, worn and dusty they were almost beyond recognition. I never knew what happened to them.

There is nothing to compare with a childhood Christmas. The waking at some unearthly hour for that wonderful moment when you looked for the presents. They were always there. The great preparations beforehand like sitting up through the night to boil the Christmas puddings in the copper. Mince pies were the size of saucers, covered in caster sugar and often washed down with a glass of Father's homemade "poison". It was an adventure to go tramping through the snow to gather the holly, ivy and mistletoe from some secret place. The snow was as fine and white as the icing on the cake. And you must never forget to make a wish whilst stirring the Christmas puddings.

Childhood Christmas treats left a great impression in my mind. The magic of hanging up a pillowcase, the feel of the sugar pig and the orange lying hidden in one corner and most of all that wonderful faith in Father Christmas.

Home from Wolverhampton, it was strange to lie in my own bed again and to listen to the weird sounds of the cut instead of the rattling trams going up the Cannock Road. Father, too, enjoyed these Christmas treats as much as I did. Before we went away he would read Dickens' *Christmas Carol* to me, the story of Scrooge and the ghosts and the sad little Tiny Tim. He was probably glad to get away from our house in case he, too, might see the spirits of Christmasses past.

Some of my thoughts of those long ago Christmasses I have put into verse:

"Always on a Christmas morn
I remember bygone years.
The music and the singing:
The laughter and the tears.

A musty smell of unused rooms
Still lingers in my nose.
The mistletoe bough, the holly bunch
With the lovely Christmas Rose.

The choir boys and the lovely crib.
The hymns and carols gay.
The smell of incense in the church:
This was my Christmas Day.

The shunting in the goods yard.
Trams rattling on their way.
All these memories I hold dear:
They made my Christmas Day.

Gas lights hissing in the street.
Houses standing in a row.
The sounds of weary trudging feet,
Quietly muffled by the snow.

Anecdotes of Christmas
Which will never go away.
Nostalgic echoes from the past
Of every Christmas Day."

Once, and only once, was I ever taken to the theatre. The disastrous occasion was a visit to the Birmingham Alexandra to see *Mother Goose*. Father's friend from Cadbury's had arranged the outing and for a special treat had booked a box.

This was wonderful. The thought of an event such as this had never even entered my head.

So close to the stage we were. So close that when an enormous man called Sammy, dressed in a striped swimsuit and carrying a bucket and spade, appeared, he was able to lift me out of the box, put me down on the stage and present me with a bucket full of goodies. It was quite a large bucket and full of sweets – the most I had ever been given!

From that moment on, I was completely stage struck and determined to become an actress. But Fate had set its seal for me. My destiny was all fixed. Ten minutes later I was removed to the "Ladies" in disgrace. The whole event had proved too much for me. I scarcely understood what all the fuss was about. After all, I had only leaned over the box and hit the violinist on the head with my spade. Perhaps that was why he wasn't too pleased! But it had been an accident . . . at least, I think it had!

CHAPTER FIVE

Halfway House

THE Halfway House was a fine old country farm with a licence to sell intoxicating drinks. It was set in pleasant surroundings with a happy, friendly atmosphere. To go inside, you passed through a small wooden gate off the towing path and crossed the farmyard. The first building on the right was the mens' toilet; beyond, there were three stables. Opposite these, on the left, was a covered barn where the animal feed was stored; and the cowsheds. A small gateway led to the pigstys and the gardens. I would climb onto the bottom half of the stable door to see what animals were inside. It might be a day-old calf with its mother. Or some newly hatched baby chicks.

I would have to hold my penny very tightly. If I lost it, I wouldn't get another. This didn't mean that I would have gone without my glass of milk, for the farmer's wife, Mrs Thompson was a very kind lady and always made me very welcome. The three Thompson boys, Ron, Ken and Doug were my nearest playmates. I didn't see very much of Mr Thompson. He was a quiet man and although I would say "hello" to him, he was usually busy serving in the bar or emerging from the cellar, jug of ale in one hand and a lighted candle in the other.

I loved my 1d glass of milk: even though it had been through the cooler, it was still slightly warm. The glass held half a pint. There was a thick foamy froth on the top; when I had drunk it all, I would have a white moustache on my upper lip.

Directly outside the house was a small covered-in courtyard with three doors leading off it. That on the left was into the living room; that facing you led to the bar parlour, taproom and staircase; and the door on the right provided access to a large, cool dairy. Outside, stood a small wooden table and bench with a water pump around the corner. Pink-flowered house leeks were massed on the low roofs of the outhouses. Chickens roamed freely in the yard, clucking and scratching away every moment of their daytime freedom. By night, they were safely fastened in the pen away from the attentions of the big, bad fox.

The Halfway House was so called because it was almost

exactly equidistant from Worcester and Birmingham, 15 miles away in each direction.

The Thompsons were hard-working, kindly country folk who would always find time to help those in need. There would be a spare stable for any boat horse that required overnight shelter. Also, plenty of fresh farm produce for the boatmen and their families. Men from all walks of life gathered in this cosy little pub for a friendly chat, a game of darts and a pint. Farmers, school teachers, Cadbury workers who came to fish the canal and reservoir, the local policeman, railway men from Aston Fields and many others.

Sammy Heath would come strolling down the cut, his camera slung over his shoulder, always ready to "snap" everything and everybody. He was a tall, broad-shouldered man with a fresh complexion and a neat little moustache. Sammy always wore a grey suit with an open-necked shirt. He walked along at a steady pace, one arm folded behind his back on which hung his folded, fawn-coloured raincoat.

Ken Thompson's horse Dobbin in the yard at the Halfway House.

Without any doubt, the star of the Halfway House was a small, thin man named Harry Bache, better known to his mates as Batchy. With his flat cloth cap, navy blue jacket and trousers and scarf tied around his neck, he reminded me of a character out of Dickens. A kind-hearted man, he wore the same clothes Winter and Summer. Without relatives and a man of few words, I vividly remember that he was extremely short-sighted. So much so, that he couldn't tell one coin from another and he held them so close to his face that I was afraid that he would push them into his eye sockets.

One great event of the school holidays was haymaking time down at the Halfway House. The grass was cut with the mowing machine. It would then lie in long, near-straight lines across the fields, waiting for the blazing sun to dry out every spot of moisture. Each day, we would walk down the canal to the farm, collect wooden rakes and set off into the field to turn the hay, making quite sure it was all dry before it was piled into small cocks. When the hay had been collected, a cart, pulled by the farm horse, would proceed slowly round the field. One of the Thompson boys led the horse, while another stacked the hay as we tossed it up to him.

When the harvest was safely gathered in, Mrs Thompson provided us all with a harvest supper in the hayfield. Nothing ever tasted as good as those harvest suppers! The warm Summer evening, the wonderful scent of the new-mown hay, the birds singing, the sweet smell of the cider, fresh bread, butter and farm cheese . . . all this made an occasion which stands out in my memory as though it happened only yesterday.

One by one, the men started to drift into the Halfway for their evening drink and to enjoy a well-earned sit down after a long and tiring day. They greeted the landlord and his wife and seated themselves around the table in the snug. Some would fill their pipes and sit there, puffing away as if they didn't have a care in the world. Others were content with a game of dominoes or darts.

I would be busy washing the dairy eggs and generally helping Mrs Thompson who was glad of a little assistance even if I only did a bit of fetching and carrying. The door to the dairy was next to the passage which led to the bar parlour. I could tell from the volume of laughter and voices that things were beginning to warm up. Any minute now, we would be hearing singing. There was always a happy atmosphere with no fighting or unpleasant scenes. Just a crowd of men out for an evening's pleasure.

Quietly and then rather more loudly, the sound of the men's harmonious voices drifted out into the still warm night. Louder and louder came the words of old ballads with haunting refrains: *Love's Old Sweet Song, Mary My Girl, Smilin' Through* and *Just a Song at Twilight.* Father always sang *In the Gloaming* and *Parted,* with the men generally joining in for the last verse. He rendered these songs with great sincerity and with so much feeling that before long he would be wiping a tear from the corner of his eye as he remembered his dearest Lassie, lying cold and lonely, but never forgotten.

As the singing died down and the men called for refills, a voice from the back would shout:

"Cum on, John. Gie us *Mary Ellen or Slap it up an' doon wi' the Whitewash Brush.*"

```
            Let the wealthy and great
            Roll in splendour and state,
            I envy them not, I declare it.
            I eat my own lamb, my own chickens and ham
            I sheer my own fleece and I wear it.
            I have lawns, I have bowers,
            I have fruits, I have flowers,
            The lark is my morning alarmer,
                    So jolly boys now
            Here's GOD, speed the plough.
            Long life and success to the Farmer.
```

"Jus' wait till I've wet me whistle and got me breath back an'
then we'll have a go."

Eventually, all good things must come to an end and with
shouts of "Goodnight" and "See you tomorrow", the men
wandered home. Some, like ourselves, had a long way to go. But
as we walked along the cutside, I was already thinking about the
following morning and all the fun there would be with another
day's haymaking. Perhaps there would be another clutch of eggs
hatched or something specially interesting to do . . . like today
when someone put a wasps' nest in a hay cock and when the man
collected the hay on his pitch fork, all the wasps swarmed out and
the poor fellow had to run for his life into the dingle and take his
trousers off. I knew who was responsible . . . but I wasn't going to
tell. Tomorrow, I might get a chance to play cricket with the boys.
Trouble is, I'm only good at fielding. Still, it's all good fun, and this
is the Summer Holidays and I don't have to go to bed early.

After a week of harvesting, the men could get very merry. But I
didn't think that Tommy Thompson's ale was as potent as Father's
home made "poison". Two or three glasses of that and you were
as "drunk as a bobhowler" or "three sheets in the wind."

On my visits to the farm I would help Mrs Thompson to milk the
cows and put the milk through the separator and the cooler.
Afterwards, I turned the churn to make the butter. The dairy was
large and cool with concrete slabs along each side where sides of
bacon would lie, curing. One day I was turning the churn when the
lid came off: fortunately, only a very small amount was wasted. I
was taught to have the greatest respect for the farmer and his
land; always to close gates; to keep the dog "to heel"; to stay on
the footpaths: and to obey all the signs. I would not have dreamed
of walking through a field of corn or uncut hay and wantonly
destroying it.

Sometimes, Mr Thompson gave us a large milk can of
"beestings". This was the first milk drawn from a newly calved
cow. When sweetened with sugar and slowly cooked in the oven,
it made a most nutritious custard.

The Halfway House was an important part of Father's life. He
would go there to drown his sorrows in Thompson's ale and
somehow managed to forget his troubles for a time with a drink
and a song. As well as being famed for his songs, he believed in the
transmigration of souls. Eric de Maré records this in his *The
Canals of England*, first published in 1950. Many of the songs had
come from coloured Bamforth picture postcards of the First

World War. If I had been Very Good, I might be allowed to look at our collection of many dozen and I memorised the verses quickly. I thought then (and still think now) that the words and illustrations of these sentimental songs were exceptionally beautiful. They were certainly extremely popular when they first appeared.

After a day running about the farm with the animals and chickens, while Father and his pals were engrossed in their singsong, we might be asked to sit down for a meal in the farmhouse kitchen with the family. A huge joint of roast beef, hot from the oven, lay on a great oval dish, running with succulent red juice and surrounded by individual Yorkshire puddings. This was enough to tempt any child's appetite . . . By the time we arrived home, I couldn't eat another morsel. Father was too sozzled with Tommy Thompson's ale to look at his dinner and Isobel would be furious. So ended the perfect day! From an early age I was used to the rumpus which followed our visits to the Halfway House. Sister's sharp tongue did not deter me.

Father handing out a 'swig of wallop' to the ice-breaker team.

CHAPTER SIX

School Days

ST Bartholomew's Church and School stand magnificently on a hill at Tardebigge, overlooking the canal. Francis Hiorn's slender tower of 1777, crowned by a needle spire soars 135 feet: a sentinel, lonely, watching and waiting. A Norman church occupied the same site in 1138. Every November 5, its bells rang out loud and clear to remind the villagers of the failure of the Gunpowder Plot. The present tower now holds three bells which are struck instead of being swung. It is said that the great bell, weighing more than half a ton, may well have caused the old tower to come crashing down into the church and destroy it on September 3, 1775. Since its rebuilding, it has been altered many times.

I attended Sunday School from the age of five. This was held in the Children's Corner. Each child was given a stamp and book with illustrations of holy days and Bible stories. It was also used as proof of attendance.

My first day at school is still clearly remembered. The snow was still crisp under my feet as I set out, clad in my warmest clothes consisting of "combs", Liberty bodice, dress, a coat made from woven blanket material and, of course, my gaiters. A two mile walk lay ahead. Clinging to my Father's hand and clutching a bag of bread and lard, I trudged through the snow wondering how I could possibly manage to remove my gaiters and put them on again once school was over, without a button hook. Once we had reached the Top Lock, it was still a long climb up Church Hill.

I really didn't think I'd get to school in time after the large dose of Syrup of Figs that Sister had forced down my throat, each drop popped in between wails and screams. The night before I had been scrubbed, rubbed, disinfected and hosed down. I reeked of quassia chips (an infusion would be used against nits) and vinegar – just in case!

After being thrust into the capable arms of the infants' teachers, Miss Wirgin and Miss Garnham, the first thing I wanted to do was "to leave the room, please, Miss." This sentence had been drilled in to me before I left home. My request was denied. After all, I had only just arrived. There was only one alternative: just sit it out with my tray of sand and string of beads.

"Let us hope and pray that Pat Warner doesn't blot her copybook on her first day at school"

I wondered what the teacher could mean.

I didn't like school. I spent most of the day standing in the corner or put outside the door: "until you cease to make that dreadful noise." The second time I was put outside, I set off for a walk among the gravestones. But who should be waiting just around the corner but the grave digger:

"I'm waiting for little girls like you who try to run away from school. Back to the classroom with you, my girl. This time it's the corner again," he said. And to the teacher:

"That's right, Missus. You watch 'er. Almost down an 'ole she wus. Us dusn't wan' 'er berid afore 'er bin edecated!"

So I was placed on the little wooden bench in front of the little wooden table, one eye on the cardboard numbers, coins, coloured chalks and small slates . . . the other eye firmly fixed upon the teacher

Our school in the churchyard.

at her large wooden desk on which rested a long wooden cane.

The school toilets were like the one at home, except that there were rows of little wooden holes to fit little bottoms. I can never remember seeing anyone empty them, so I concluded they must reach for ever. Neither can I recall seeing a toilet for the teachers. Maybe they never went. At least, not during school hours.

In 1800, Miss Sarah Hemming kept the Magpie public house which stood in the churchyard, close to the church. Almost twenty years later it was closed and converted into a school, possibly the first National School in the parish. This building was demolished in 1843 and two schools and a house built as a replacement. This was all due to the generosity of Lady Harriet Clive. For many years it was known as The Earl of Plymouth's School, Tardebigge.

At the entrance to the churchyard on our way in to school, was the tomb of the Queen of the Gipsies who departed this life in the year 1832. It was a huge tomb, covered with cracks and joints. We would stand with our ears pressed against it, listening and waiting . . .

More than one hundred children attended the school in 1929. Mr and Mrs Dilkes lived at the school house. He was Headmaster, assisted by his wife. Mrs Badger taught the middle class. The very first song I learned was:

> "Mr Dilkes is a very good man.
> He goes to church on Sundays.
> He prays to God to give him strength
> To wallop the kids on Mondays."

And cane us he did. But, to be fair, we always deserved it. His pride and joy was a model railway, displayed in the garden at the back of the school. As well as plenty of discipline at home we had the village Policeman to keep us on the straight and narrow. Every Saint's Day and Holy Day we attended church. We had our own banner and marched to church singing:

> "Brightly gleams our banner
> Pointing to the sky,
> Waving on Christ's soldiers
> To their home on high.
> Marching through the desert
> Gladly thus we pray,
> Still with hearts united,
> Singing on our way."

Mothering Sunday was celebrated with the usual Sunday service and each child picked a bunch of wild flowers for their mother. If I remembered, I gave mine to my Sister. Each Good Friday, we sang *The Story of the Cross* from beginning to end. Not one verse was ever left out. It was, indeed, very moving. On odd occasions at a church service, I offered to "blow" the hand-pumped organ. It was jolly good exercise. The trouble was, if I stopped, the organ wheezed to a halt. The original instrument was a barrel organ which was moved from the gallery to the chancel in 1878. Electric blowing was not introduced until 1951.

Mr Liddle was organist when I was in the Infants' School. A very tall, slim man, he always wore a fawn raincoat, open-toed sandals without socks, a short sleeved shirt and khaki shorts, Summer and Winter. On reflection, he was oddly suspicious.

Without any doubt, the year's most emotive service was on Armistice Day, November 11. This was to honour those who had given their lives in the Great War. We all lined up for a big parade and every man, woman and child wore a 1d poppy with pride. The procession was led by the Vicar, followed by the choir, with one choirboy holding the church banner. Other banners were carried by the British Legion, the Scouts and Guides and other dignitaries of the parish. The hymns were the same each year; *God of our Fathers, Known of Old* and *O Valiant Hearts, Who to You Glory Came.*

After the hymns came the prayers and the Two Minute Silence. This produced a deathly hush, with only the sound of the wind howling and the cry of a lonely bird high above our heads. As we bowed in silence, my mind was filled with pictures of the "Tommies" sitting in the trenches and all those who never returned to "dear old Blighty". And I remembered lines from my treasured postcards, illustrating the songs of the Great War. I recalled Rupert Brooke's poem, *The Soldier:*
"If I should die, think only this of me:
That there's some corner of a foreign field
That is forever England . . ."
Many games were enjoyed in the school playground: "Poor Mary sits a-weeping", "Wallflowers", "Sheep Sheep Come Home", Green Gravel", "Nebuchadnezar", "The Farmer's in the Dell", "The Wind, the Wind, the Wind Blows High", "Here we Go Round the Mulberry Bush", "What's the Time, Mr Wolf?" and "Statues", which cost me a piece of a front tooth.

We played Shinty (hockey), Netball, Rounders, Hop Scotch,

My teachers in September 1930. Left to right: *Mrs Dilkes, Mr Dilkes, Miss Garnham, the Rev. Scott-Warren and Miss Wirgin.*

Whip and Top, Conkers, Yo-Yo and Jacky Five Stones. We also had PT and went for swimming lessons at Redditch Baths.

On May 1, we danced around a Maypole and plaited the gaily coloured ribbons. May 24 was the old Empire Day when we gathered beneath the Union Jack and sang *Flag of our Country, Flag of our King* and other patriotic songs.

When Mr Dilkes retired, Mr A T Knight was appointed Headmaster, assisted by Mrs Badger. Mrs Eades joined the school in 1931. Mrs Mountford came a bit later. The top classroom was divided into two separate classes by means of folding doors. School milk was served at the lunch break. We took sandwiches for the midday meal. Mine were either bread and jam, bread and lard or bread and treacle. Some days I might swap a sandwich with a friend. Other people's tuck always tasted better than your own!

There was a large barn in the playground where we could shelter during break if it rained. In here, we could play skipping games like "Salt, Mustard, Vinegar, Pepper" and practice jumping over the rope until the bell clanged to summon us back to our lessons. On cold days it was nice to sit in the cloakroom and enjoy our sandwiches in luxury by the warm pipes. We would then put on our coats and spend the remainder of break in the playground.

We had plenty of homework to occupy the evenings – all done by lamplight and a cosy open fire. Poetry was my favourite. No matter the number of verses, once copied, I could remember it word for word.

At Tardebigge School there was always something to distract one's attention away from the blackboard. Outside, in the churchyard, there would be a succession of daily happenings: funerals, weddings, Christenings or just people walking about. Many were the times that I felt the teacher's hand laid firmly on my head to focus my gaze once more in the right direction.

Once, the class was told to model in clay some small item which they had seen in Hewell Grange on the night of the village children's party (Chapter Eight). A vase, a bust, some type of ornament, anything. For my model, I chose a little naked cherub . . . complete in all his anatomy. The teacher went very red in the face and started to splutter. She was quite horrified! I just could not understand why she wasn't very pleased with my effort. For my part, it was the first time I had seen a nude male. I assumed that all cherubs were born with two long legs and a short one. I wondered why my model wasn't put on display with the others. After all, it was lifelike.

Mrs Mountford kept us all spellbound reading Rudyard Kipling's *Just So* stories and the tale about Epaminondas, whose Mammy used to say "Yo aint got the sense yo was born wid".

Mr Knight taught us to appreciate good music and songs. We learned *The Faery Song* from *The Immortal Hour; Where ere You Walk; Sweet Polly Oliver; Sea Fever; Lizzy Lindsay; The Sweet Nightingale; Oh Shepherd Boy; Rolling Down to Rio;* various cantatas and many others.

We had History, Geography, English, Cookery, Gardening, Needlework and Arithmetic. There were inkwells on the desks, poster paints, potato cuts, flour and water for paste ... What more could we ask for?

Friday was Cookery and Laundry day, for girls of 12 and over, with lessons held in the Village Hall. Our teacher was Mrs Frisby. During our dinner break, we would walk along the Donkey Hole to the Post Office at the Old Wharf to buy a halfpenny or even a farthing bar of Black Jack Toffee, two Aniseed Balls or a Bull's Eye. If there was time, we might go back across the Shaws, a field used by the boat people to lead their horses from the Old Wharf to the New, while their boats were being taken through Tardebigge Tunnel.

Autograph books were a great favourite. My friends and relations could invariably oblige with a verse. Funny verses some of them were:

> "The boy stood on the burning deck,
> His feet were all in blisters.
> He split his trousers down the back
> And had to wear his sister's."
> Or:
> "Out in the mighty ocean
> Not a tram car was in sight.
> The sun and the moon shone brightly
> And it rained all day that night.
> Yet in that Summer snow storm
> The moon shone just like glass,
> And a bare-footed boy with shoes on
> Stood sitting on the grass."

It didn't take long to fill a small book and a very prized possession it was, kept under the pillow at night. You never know, someone might well borrow it and copy out all those exclusive verses.

Collecting cigarette cards was a great hobby. Much fun was to be had swapping them with your friends. I was rather lucky, because the fishermen would save them for me.

In 1935, we took part in the Inter-Schools Music Festival, held in the Pump Room at Royal Leamington Spa. Our chosen song was *This England*, John of Gaunt's speech, from *King Richard II*:

> "This royal throne of kings, this scepter'd isle
> This earth of majesty, this seat of Mars,
> This other Eden, demi-paradise;
> This fortress built by Nature for herself
> Against infection and the hand of war;
> This happy breed of men, this little world;
> This precious stone set in the silver sea,
> Which serves it in the office of a wall,
> Or as a moat defensive to a house,
> Against the envy of less happier lands;
> This blessed plot, this earth, this realm, this
>   England."

The Village Dick Wittington. *I am the fairy on the extreme left.*

It was exciting to be taken by coach all the way to Leamington. To have 2d (0.8p) to spend on an ice cream. The girls wore white dresses, white socks and white pumps; the boys white shirts and dark trousers. We felt it was a great honour.

It was a thrilling day when, at the age of about 11, I was chosen to play the part of one of the fairies in the Rev. Scott Warren's Christmas Pantomime, *Dick Whittington*. There were numerous rehearsals, costume fittings and work on the scenery and lighting. Performances were staged in our own Tardebigge Village Hall and ran for almost a week. I wore a superb white crêpe paper dress, a tinsel crown and wings trimmed with silver. The warmth and the applause was wonderful, but it was a long walk home after each performance, dark and scaring as we listened to our footsteps echoing in the empty locks.

We had our Girl Guide meetings at the Village Hall. I was in the Pimpernel Patrol. Afterwards, I would walk home alone by the canal late at night. I would be a little frightened, but not as much as the little water voles I disturbed and which jumped into the water with a loud "plop". I was meant to wait for my Father to meet me, but if we finished early I would start off on my own. I knew he would be very cross, but there were never any objectionable characters lurking about.

Music festivals were frequently held in the church and one piece well loved by choir and congregation was *Hark, hark the Lark at Heaven's Gate Sings*. One rousing and patriotic song was:

> "It comes from the Misty Ages,
> The banner of England's might.
> The blood red cross
> Of the brave St George
> That burns on a field of white."

The lament of James II when exiled from England, brought tears to our eyes:

> "Farewell Manchester. Noble town farewell.
> Here with loyalty every breast shall swell.
> Where so ere I roam, here as in a home,
> Ever dear Manchester, my own true home."

One of the first things expected of me from the moment I started school, was to put flowers on my Mother's grave. There were no ifs or buts. From a very early age, I had known exactly where in the churchyard she was buried. I also knew what it meant to be buried, as I had seen my Father dispose of a ferret which had suddenly died. Mother's grave was at the foot of the new churchyard, alongside the wooden railings. My sisters, who had died before I was born, were also buried there somewhere, but I never discovered where. A large yew tree stood by the side of the grave, tall and straight, only moving when a good strong wind bowed it towards the canal. Father vowed that it nodded to him as a reminder that he was still remembered by his "Lassie".

As I knelt there, beside the huge mound of earth, with the knees of my stockings soaking up the dew in the grass, I wondered exactly what lay beneath. All impressions of my Mother were based on a photograph taken with Father at Christmas 1924: it hung on the wall of the living room; and the old gramophone record of *The faery Dream Boat*. Listening to this lullaby and looking at the picture gave me my Mother's portrait and her voice. What more could I ask for?

> "The faery dream boat in the harbour
> Anchored to a white moonbeam.
> All the crew are waiting for you.
> They're ready to sail, so hurry up do!
> Soon you'll be of to dreamland,
> Over the mighty sea.
> And when the night is through,
> The Captain and his crew
> Will bring you back to Daddy and me."

Did she still look like the picture on the wall, with those almond-shaped eyes? Or is she lying there with her hands folded across her chest like Jairus' daughter on the Sunday School stamp? Or is she just sleeping? No one ever tells me these things, so how am I supposed to know what is going on beneath this hard clay?

I would try to make the jam jar stand up in the hole I had poked out with a piece of wood. But the clay was very hard and the wood kept breaking. I had to fetch water from a tap by the path in the old churchyard. It was fixed onto a stump of wood and was quite difficult to turn on and off. If I didn't put plenty of water in the jar, the flowers would die. I wonder, will someone bury these also? I must hurry up before the grave digger catches me: he'll think I am

Tardebigge School, 1936.

playing truant again and drag me back to school . . . I would wander along the path towards the church, dragging the heavy watering can, which must always be returned to its hook by the tap. Then I would stand for a few seconds, day-dreaming – as usual. Even though I had never known my sisters, I wondered which part of the cemetery they were resting in. My brother John was buried somewhere near the tap in unconsecrated ground, it was said, as he had not been Christened. On one occasion, I was suddenly aware that someone was watching me. I looked up into the face of a very tall man, dressed in black. I thought that I'd seen that face in church on a Sunday.

"Hello, little girl," he said. "You're a very little girl to be wandering around here alone. Have you been putting flowers on a grave?"

"Yes, sir. On my Mother's grave."

"Have you any brothers and sisters?"

"Yes, sir. They're all here except one."

"All? How many is all?"

"Well, sir, They tell me it would be seven."

"Ah well. I must put these flowers on my dear wife's grave. She died last week. Goodbye, little girl. Hurry home."

"Bye, sir."

I'm sure I did right to call him 'sir'. Father said that if he wore a hat it was 'sir'; but if he wore a cap it was plain 'Mister'.

As I wandered home by the cutside, I was thinking that everywhere I went, I always heard about death. At home and in the churchyard. Yet no one had ever explained to me. A few lines of a poem flashed through my mind: words that had made a tremendous impression on me:

We are Seven by William Wordsworth
"A simple Child,
That lightly draws its breath,
And feels its life in every limb,
What should it know of death?

"Sisters and brothers, little Maid,
How many may you be?"
"How many? Seven in all," she said
And wondering looked at me.

"And when the ground was white with snow,
And I could run and slide,
My brother John was forced to go,
and he lies by her side."

"But they are dead; these two are dead!
Their spirits are in heaven!"
'Twas throwing words away; for still
The little Maid would have her will,
And said, "Nay, we are seven!"

There was no doubt about it, poetry was the love of my life. But teacher would say:
"Get on with you sums, girl."
"Don't want to do sums. I want to be a nurse."
"Useless wooden-headed girl! You'll never do any good at all."
"You don't have to do sums to be a nurse. You just have to put your cool hand on the soldier's brow, like the lady on the card. You know, on the postcard."
"Silly girl. Be quiet!" The teacher was getting quite angry.
"I'm going to be a District Nurse and ride a bicycle along the towing path by my canal," I announced, defiantly.
"I suppose you will visit all *four* of the cottages?" Under my breath I muttered:
"Silly old thing. Trouble with her, she has no imagination."
I wished that someone would listen to me. 'Nurse' was a dirty word at home and I wasn't allowed to discuss the subject. I wished I knew why.

CHAPTER SEVEN

My Heroine

DURING my walks to Bromsgrove and back, I often used to see the District Nurse pedalling around in her black stockings and black below-the-knees bloomers. This woman was my idol. I used to dream about her and all the little babies she carried in a black Gladstone bag, strapped to the back of her bicycle.

"I will be a District Nurse, one day. You'll see." I broke this news very gently to Father, because my big ears had heard one day that my eldest sister, Eva, had been a trained nurse in a mental institution. She had worked under appalling conditions and died at the age of 22. Father was not happy at the prospect of another nurse in the family.

"A wooden headed wench like you be a nurse? Pigs might fly with their tails cocked up! You'll never be any good as long as your behind hangs downhill. You might turn out to be a scholastic disaster, but that's about all!" Father was not encouraging.

So many times I learned my lessons in humility. But one day... one day I would show them! I too would ride a bicycle and carry a black bag and I would wear black stockings *and* black bloomers (if necessary). Nothing or anyone on this earth would prevent me from entering the nursing profession. I would be like the Voluntary Aid Detachment Nurse on the *Queen of the Earth* postcard.

I treasured those First World War pictorial song cards much more than any children's book. They were so real to me, with each card illustrating a verse of a patriotic song. Father would bounce me on his knee until my teeth rattled as he sang the songs to me. He put so much action and feeling into them that the songs almost came alive. I would string the titles together to make up my very own story:

I would visualise the Tommies... *Somewhere in France without you*, looking *Across the Sands of Time* to *Where the Black-Eyes Susans Grow* thinking that *Just for Tonight* they could *Let the Great Big World Keep Turning* and even although *The Wide Seas Roll Between Us God Guard You Till We Meet Again* because *There's a Ship that's Bound for Blighty* which will *Take Me Back to Dear Old Blighty* so *God Be With You Till We*

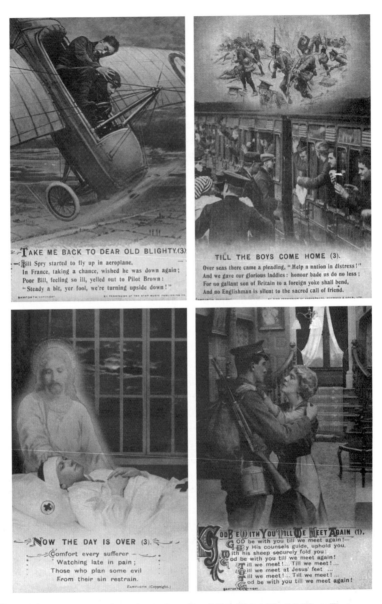

Four of my treasured song postcards of the First World War. There was a different colour picture for each verse.

Meet Again I Shall Come Home When the Ebb Tide Flows and see
my *Queen of the Earth Now the Day is Over God Keep you in His
Care* and so *Sweet Adeline My Dream of Delight If I Could Turn
the Clock Back* you could *Show Me the Way to Your Heart.
Remember, There's a Friend in Every Milestone so Lead Kindly
Light* and show me *The Roses of Picardy.* Until then remember
Till the Boys Come Home. I shall think of *The Rosary* and *The
Holy City* and be *Nearer My God to Thee.* He only takes *The
Bravest, the Best.* So, *Joan of Arc, They are Calling You* and
When I Lost You, That was the End Of My *Dream . . .*
    Thirty songs which are just as alive in my memory now as they
were more than fifty years ago. I lay in bed, imagining the
Tommies in the trenches: they too were dreaming, thinking of the
train for London town, fed up with apple and plum jam,
remembering the grey-haired mother all alone on the quay and all
those that kept the home fires burning.
    I imagined all the troopships, the huge German warships and
the Zeppelins, making a strange droning as they soared among the
clouds. The empty brass shell cases in the hearth could have told
many stories, had they been able to talk. Most of all, I liked the
card with the VAD nurse, wearing her apron with a large red cross:

"In every heart she has fashioned her throne.
As Queen of the Earth, she reigneth alone."

I wondered if I would ever be like her, my fairy queen. I could see
her every night as soon as I closed my eyes. There she was
standing at the head of my bed, placing her cool hand on my brow,
watching over me like a guardian angel. Telling me that there was
something she wanted me to do, when I had stopped being a little
girl. One day, you'll see. I'll show them. I, too, "will reign alone."
    Whether it was our own District Nurse with her black
bloomers, my Mother, who had been a children's nanny or my
sister Eva, the mental nurse, that inspired me, I'll never know. But
I still have a secret feeling that it was the VAD Nurse with the red
cross on her bosom that was responsible. Little did I then realise
that 1939 would find me dressed in the St John Ambulance
uniform, nursing voluntarily at Bromsgrove Public Assistance
Infirmary, otherwise known as The Workhouse. I was thrown in at
the deep end and enjoyed every minute of it.
    A Tardebigge District Nursing Association was formed in
January 1930 and was disbanded in September 1946 prior to the

The VAD Nurse that launched me on my career.

commencement of the National Health Service. My colleague, District Nurse Caroline Hirons, has kindly made available the Association's minute book, and certain extracts are well worth repeating here. Officers and Committee members comprised various landowners of the parish, business men and women and the Vicar. In the latter years, the Countess of Plymouth was President.

My Father told me about these Committee meetings with his customary words of wisdom:

"Be warned, my wench. Never get mixed up with them there Committee meetings. You won't know if you are on foot or on horseback by the time they have finished with you. When you become a student nurse, you'll get 18s lld (94p) a month, and you won't even have enough to pay your bus fare home, always supposing you get given the day off."

How right he was! But I had to find these things out for myself – the hard way.

As far back as I can remember there was always talk in the house, at the bus stops and in the shops about the Hewell Nursing Association and 'having in the Nurse'. Where the Nurse had been, and what she had done and why were never explained to me:

"You don't want your Pat to 'ear, but ol' Mrs So and So, you know. Her's bin laid out . . .

"Oh, is her dead then?"

The Hewell Nursing Association was formed in 1894 to provide resident nurses at a low fee to regular subscribers.

At an early meeting at the Tardebigge District Nursing Association, maternity fees were fixed at 21s ($1.05) to 42s ($2.10) according to circumstances. All members were entitled to the free services of the Nurse, with non members paying 2s 6d (12½p) for the first visit and 1s (5p) per visit thereafter. A District Nurse was appointed in January 1930 at an annual salary of $180 together with board, lodging, laundry, uniform and a rather heavy sit-up and-beg bicycle. The Nurse was introduced to the Committee and asked to attend meetings each month, to give a detailed report of her work. From this, it appears that she was paying about 300 visits a month.

On one occasion the secretary reported that Mrs X had come to live in the district, joined the Association, had a baby and then ceased to pay her subscriptions. In effect, she had had her baby for 4s 4d (22p)!

Matters over which the Committee endlessly deliberated now seem very insignificant. Should the Nurse's bicycle be repaired at a cost of 10s (50p) or should she have a new one for £3? For a long while, it was hoped to provide her with a car. Later, she asked for a new bicycle saddle. The matter of the car was postponed indefinitely. A shawl was presented to the Association to be raffled: would contributions collectors sell tickets at 3d (1.25p) each?

After Nurse had been in the post for twelve months, she announced that she intended to purchase a motor bicycle. What help could she expect regarding expenses? After a drawnout discussion, it was agreed to offer her £5 a year extra plus road tax and comprehensive insurance. It was pointed out that Nurse would anyway be using the machine for her own pleasure and amusement. Next, comes an entry that Nurse has been involved in an accident on her motor bike. She took a long period of sick leave and then decided to resign. The replacement found the motor bike too heavy to handle, so a new pushbike was acquired for £2-2s (£2.10).

In 1935, a special meeting was convened to discuss purchase of a car for Nurse. After a lengthy discussion, a Committee member announced he had already bought the vehicle. Various fund-raising events were planned to defray expenses. The Rowney Green Shakespearean Society gave a performance of *A Midsummer Night's Dream* in Hewell Park with tickets at 3s, 2s, and 1s (15p 10p and 5p). This raised a total of £8. A Whist Drive brought in £2. It was proposed that Nurse be allowed two gallons of petrol per week, at a cost of about £1-16s (£1.80) for three months. Shortly afterwards, Nurse resigned.

When the Association was wound up in 1946, together with most other voluntary health organisations, the then Nurse was presented with a shopping bag and a cheque for £25.

CHAPTER EIGHT

Hewell

THE highlight of the school year was the annual Christmas Party given by the Rt Hon Ivor Miles, Earl of Plymouth, accompanied by the Countess of Plymouth and their children. Everyone in the school was invited to this breath-taking event, which was held at the Plymouth mansion, Hewell Grange.

Several days beforehand, a van would arrive at the school from Hewell and a number of wicker laundry baskets would be unloaded. These contained the magic carpet slippers for the children to wear in the ballroom and prevent the floor from being damaged. Shoes and slippers with hard soles or any type of footwear which might have sprigs (little hob-nails) were definitely not allowed. Most of our parents could not afford to buy soft shoes specially for us,

The majority of slippers were tied in pairs, those for the girls with ankle straps, while the boys wore conventional bedroom slippers. We dived headfirst into the hampers, all very eager to get fitted out. It was like trying on the most beautiful pair of ballet shoes. We would dance and pirouette until we were quite giddy. Then it was down to earth with a bump as the teacher's voice reminded us that we still had lessons to do:

"Children, put your slippers safely away in your pump bags."

Imagine putting those lovely slippers in with those awful black pumps!

"What's the matter with you, Freddie? You've got your slippers, I don't know why you are making that fuss. Oh, goodness me! Take them off at once. They're odd ones and one foot is bigger than the other. Now, I wonder who can have the other odd pair?"

Would the great day never come? I was much too excited to stand still to have my first party dress fitted. There were numerous visits to my Aunt for fittings, a process that involved sticking pins into me as well as the dress! Aunt had discovered a piece of pink *crêpe de Chine*, left over from bygone days. Also a beautiful length of thick reversible pink satin ribbon six inches in width. The night before the great day, I was scrubbed and polished and my hair washed and tied in curling rags. Next morning, half an hour after it had been brushed, it was as straight as a poker. Nevertheless, like Cinderella, I went to the Ball.

It was very cold on that day in January 1930 as we set off on the long walk from school to Hewell Grange. Down School Lane, across the main road, through the first Lodge Gates and along the long drive which led to the Carriage Drive. Through the large carriage doors and into a covered courtyard with a stone floor. Here, we placed our shoes and outdoor clothing on trestle tables. A large number of staff were there to greet us. After we had put on our party slippers, we formed two long columns and proceeded along a winding passage that led to the Ballroom. A thick carpet was laid down the centre of the marble floor of the passage. Halfway along, we went down six steps and continued until we reached another flight of steps leading directly into the Great Hall, better known to us as the Ballroom.

Large decorative jars stood on the floor of the passage, together with marble busts, and alabaster Cupid figurines. Oil portraits and tapestries hung on the pannelled walls. It was all very awe-inspiring, but we had no time to stand and stare:

"Come along now, children! Don't dawdle. The party will be over before you get into the Hall."

My first impression of the Great Hall was that I must be dreaming. This couldn't be the school party I had heard so much about. It must be fairyland! Shimmering lights were reflected in the oak pannelling. There were dozens of bronze figures and white ancestoral busts. Pretty stones, like coloured stars, winked at me from the ceiling, making reflections in the mirror-like floor. A huge fireplace stood on one side of the room. I gazed at it, thinking that Father Christmas could easily get down that one. A large silver bed stood at one end together with a massive dolls' house belonging to Lady Gillian, the daughter of the house.

We used that floor like skaters on an ice rink, sliding up and down until we were out of breath. We danced, played games and the children of the house showered us from above with crackers and balloons. The staff stood along the landings and galleries, watching our activities.

Each child received a present from the Earl and his family. We all sat cross-legged on the floor. As our names were called out in turn, we would walk up the Hall and accept the gift with a polite "Thank you" and a curtsy from the girls and a bow from the boys.

Tired and breathless, we all trooped back along the corridors to the courtyard to wrap up in our warm clothes and to change into

Hewell Grange.

our shoes. The great wooden doors were propped open, and, as each child walked into the cold night air, we were handed a bag containing a big iced bun, an apple, an orange and an assortment of sweets.

Parents were waiting outside to collect their offspring and it was a tired and weary band of travellers that wound their way through Hewell Park and into the loneliness of the night.

The bright lights of the party were now just a small twinkle in the distance.

The present Hewell Grange which I knew and loved, was built between 1884 and 1891. The stone was brought from the Runcorn Quarries in Cheshire by canal and then carried by horse-drawn tramway to the site, where it was cut up. From the beginning, the house was wired for electricity. There was also a form of central heating, known as the Plenum System of the Movement of Air. Fresh air would be drawn through vents in the walls and convected into the boiler room, coal then being very cheap. The resulting warm air was circulated around the house and released into each room via narrow grills above the oak pannelling. Air finally escaped through a 12ft diameter copper dome set in the roof.

I was fascinated by the tapestries covering the walls of the Great Hall. To me, they were just like enormous pictures. I was not to know that they were copies of the Bussac Tapestries which hang in the Cluny Museum in Paris. The little teak staircase, connecting downstairs offices with the bathroom and bedroom corridor, had been brought from Lord Clive's house in India.

Lady Plymouth's Sitting Room ceiling featured a maze in the Italian style, painted in gold and blue. Silk used in some of the furnishings was woven at Hewell, while some of the timber used was cut from oaks in the Park.

The Chapel is very fine, with a carved wooden ceiling copied from the Accademia in Venice. Below, is a marble frieze in the form of cherubs' faces, each one different. Stained glass windows depict the Presentation of the Charter of the Bordesley Abbey Land and St George and the Dragon. The then Earl was deeply interested in glass work, creating all the window designs himself and having them made in the Hewell glass studio by Alfred Pike.

Until the Dissolution, Hewell was the Grange, or Home Farm, of Bordesley Abbey. The land passed to Lord Windsor and a Queen Anne style mansion was built there by Other, Second Lord Plymouth, in 1716. But the nature of the crumbling sandstone and its situation near a lake forced dismantling and partial demolition in 1881. The remaining elevation and portico was known to me as The Old Ruins. It provided the grandiose setting for our school production in the open air of *A Midsummer Night's Dream.*

Weather permitting, Strawberry Teas were held at the foot of the terraces leading up the Water Tower standing on the top of Planted Hill. We had a wonderful time running down the steep banks and getting lost in the maze. White quartz chippings covered the paths. Probably refuse from the tin mines, they had been brought from Cornwall in 1904 entirely by water: Bristol Channel, Gloucester & Sharpness Canal, River Severn and Worcester & Birmingham Canal. The Water Tower was used to power the lifts in the Grange and also to work the garden fountains. A small wooden building near the edge of the lake contained pumping equipment, to keep the Tower supplied. With its dull thumping sound, it was known as "The Ram".

Sunday afternoons were frequently spent walking in Hewell Park. I liked Autumn best, when the wind was blowing and there were deep piles of leaves for me to "scuff" through. We could collect sweet chestnuts to take home and roast on the fire. Sometimes, we would meet the Earl of Plymouth with his children and he would pass the time of day with my Father.

May 1937 saw the Coronation of King George VI and Queen

The Old Ruins, all that remained of the early 18th century mansion.

Opposite: *Victorian garden design at its most complicated and labour-intensive! At the centre is a pool with Italian fountain. No wonder Hewell was a popular provider of local employment* Right: *my paper Yeomen of the Guard outfit, being modelled on the lockside by our house.*

Elizabeth. A great party was held in Hewell Park with all the usual festivities. Bunting and flags flew everywhere. The men had their Tug O' War; a Treasure Hunt took place. For the children there were egg and spoon races, three-legged races and many more. The Fancy Dress Competition attracted a large entry. I was dressed as a Yeoman of the Guard, constructed from coloured crêpe paper. My Sister took the design from a cigarette card picture. Considering the nature of the occasion, my costume was particularly appropriate. It was a very happy day. The sun shone down on everyone and we listened on the radio to the broadcast from London, hearing all the people cheering as they lined the streets. We were unable to catch the whole programme, as it was a long walk home to Hewell. At school we embroidered samplers to mark the event and these were put in a special competition. Each child received a photograph of the King and Queen and the Princesses. Father was really pleased by this, as he was very much a "true blue" Royalist.

The Earl of Plymouth who came to our school parties and many other events was Ivor Miles, created Earl of Plymouth, May 1 1923. Born in 1889, he died in 1943 and rests in Tardebigge churchyard at the site of the Vacant Chair. Afterwards, the estate was sold off to defray death duties and Hewell Grange was taken over by the War Office. It is now H M Borstal Training Centre.

There had always been a tremendous bond between the Hewell Estate and the Tardebigge villagers. The 'big house' was a way of life with its close-knit community and opportunities for employment. Workers included a full domestic staff, coachmen, grooms, gardeners, dairy hands, farm labourers, wood-cutters, blacksmiths and wheelwrights. Many of the young people who worked there were the children of canal lock keepers and maintenance staff. Frank Colledge was a hall boy at the age of 16, while my eldest sister had been a seamstress.

I suppose that the break up of the Estate was inevitable. Tardebigge was never quite the same afterwards.

The Old House Hewell now known as, 'The Old Ruins'.

CHAPTER NINE

Life Around The Reservoir

OUR house backed onto Tardebigge Reservoir. It had been constructed from a great pit left after clay was extracted for making bricks for the canal bridges, locks and culverts. When the canal was completed, the Company decided to make a reservoir of the site and for storing water in the days of heavy commercial traffic it was to prove invaluable. During thunder storms, water levels could rise with great rapidity. Rainy weather over the Lickey Hills would soon fill the canal's summit level and any surplus would be run to the Reservoir via a culvert that began near the Top Lock and ran past the Dial Houses, under the London Lane, past the back of the Engine House and into the Reservoir behind George Bate's garden. Upper Bittell and Tardebigge were considered to be the canal's main reservoirs, with additional water supplies coming from Harbourne, Lifford, Lower Bittell, Cofton, and Wychall.

Father would sometimes be required to remain on night duty, ready for a spell of water running if his brother Will should telephone from the Top Lock. First signs of trouble were flooding in the Upper Bittell and Cofton reservoirs. A large volume of water running down to Lower Bittell would eventually be too much for the sluices, weirs and side pounds to accept. Overflowing could then result, with the possibility of breached banks.

There was a small reservoir at the Halfway Bridge, Lock 41, in constant use around 1910. If a large number of boats were expected to work down the canal (bringing water supplies with them) the lock keeper would run any surplus to the Halfway. Here, it could be useful in helping craft coming up from Worcester, especially if they were heavily laden. It was part of a lock keeper's job to keep an accurate record of rainfall and the rise and fall of the canal levels.

Water running entailed a good deal of concentration. Back paddles would be opened on the sluicegates to allow flood water to escape. A huge volume then rushed through culverts into a ditch that ran from Tardebigge, through the fields at the back of the Engine House, down into the Reservoir and out again via storm paddles into the Dingle. Equally important as releasing surplus waste was not to let too much go.

I have often stood on the Reservoir bank when the water was running. You could hear it roaring underground and feel the vibration beneath your feet. Having reached the Dingle, the water continued its journey past the Halfway House, until it eventually reached the Five Mile Pound at Astwood Lock and the foot of the 'Thirties'.

The day after a night of water running involved a good long walk down the canal to check the locks. The air would be fresh and the canal surface topped with mounds of light brown foam, a bit like the 'head' on Tommy Thompson's ale. If I wasn't at school, I enjoyed helping wind up the paddles and open or close the gates. Perhaps it was all the Scott's Emulsion that had been poured down me, for I was regularly using a windlass, chopper, axe and saw, all before I was six years old.

In 1916, my Father accepted the position of water bailiff for the Bourneville Angling Club. His salary was £3 per annum, rising to £10 in 1930. Duties included selling fishing tickets to members and their friends at a cost of between 2s 6d (12½) and 5s (25p) a year and 10s after 1930. These amounts were deducted from members' wages at the factory. Day permits could be bought for 1s 6d (7½p). A small flat-bottomed punt with two oars was moored near our house for the use of fishermen and our family. Both boat and oars had been made from timber from the Hewell Estate which was taken to the Tardebigge New Wharf sawmill and fashioned by the local carpenter, George Bate. I spent many carefree hours sitting in that punt, hiding beneath the tree which hung over the water's edge, escaping from Isobel and the everlasting washing up which seemed to haunt me so much.

At certain times of the year fresh stocks of fish were brought by road to ensure that the angling remained satisfactory. When Father retired in 1950, his Cadbury payment had risen to £20 a year.

During the fishing season, there was never a dull moment. Father was busy issuing fishing tickets and Isobel making jugs of tea (at 6d – 2½p – per jug) to say nothing of gallons of pop, selling for 2d (0.8p) a bottle. The long, sunny days produced a good thirst among the anglers. Some of the men were local people who came to fish the canal and enjoy a day out in the open with their wives and children. Not everyone, however, was there for the fishing. Mr and Mrs H Fox kept their caravan by the path that led to Patchett's Farm. I was made very welcome at this, their weekend home. Mr and Mrs C Holmes brought their Scout troop and sons Bob and Peter: they camped near the Reservoir bank. Many of the regulars were Cadbury employees from Bournville. Tommy Arms came along on his bicycle. A young couple arrived on a tandem. There were Mr and Mrs Bennett, Mr and Mrs Cleaver, Karl Veyke, Jack Hobbs and the Heaton, Henshaw, Hazelwood and Hobbis families. And there was dear old Mr Jones, who always wore a most beautiful calceolaria in his buttonhole. I would wonder why the flower never faded, for it was just as fresh after his day's fishing as when he had arrived.

He was so proud of his calceolaria, growing them himself in a little greenhouse. One day, my friend Mr Jones was in our house and removed his jacket, placing it on the sofa, before paying a visit up the garden path. This is my chance, I thought . . . and on the back of the lapel there was a little metal water-filled tube with a tiny cork at the top through which poked the stem of the flower.

Three Cadbury anglers in the Reservoir punt.

How very clever! Now I knew the secret of Mr Jones' fresh flower. But it really did have the most strange smell!

There was another dear old gentleman who came most weeks to the house for a meal. Before he sat down to the table, he removed his false teeth and carefully placed them on our copy of the *Radio Times* on the open end of the sofa. He then covered them with his trilby hat. So, in rushes the 'Little Horror', tired and hot, leaps bodily on the sofa with her accustomed finesse, and up in the air shoot the trilby, closely followed by the teeth! I dashed out of the front door without waiting for the inevitable threats. For once, I was seen but not heard.

Quite often, members of the Angling Club Committee paid Father a visit: Mr J H Herbert, the Honorary Secretary, and Mr A J Turner, who was one of Father's closest friends.

Some of the fishermen would camp out at the weekends, their motto being 'early to bed, early to rise'. I would awake to the sounds of their voices drifting across the Reservoir on a fine sunny morning and I knew that it would be another busy and exciting day. Some preferred to stay the night in our house and I would hear them spinning yarns long after I was tucked up in bed. Mal Drinkwater, young Harold Jones and Ronnie Morris regularly stayed with us. There were lots of other Cadbury employees who came to the Reservoir, whose names I never knew. I walked a good many miles around the banks, carrying jugs of tea and bottles of pop to thirsty fishermen.

One day, there was terrific excitement. One of the fishermen had arrived with his family in an Austin Seven car. What is more, he actually brought it over the bridge and drove down the towpath to our front door. It was unheard of in the 1930s . . . and in front of our house, too! I was eight years old when this phenomenon arrived, but nothing in this world would induce me to sit inside. I surveyed the monster fearfully, wishing it would hurry up and vanish from sight . . . equally, it *was* a novelty not to be missed. It might be years before we had a close-up like this again.

When the car eventually moved, the noise was appalling and the smell of the fumes even worse. I hoped they wouldn't bring that horrible thing here again. Surely, there must be something I could do to keep it away? I could try praying:

"Dear God, I think that I am a good girl. I say my prayers each night and I don't ask for much. If you will stop them bringing that awful smelly thing I will never ever again say 'haymen, straw women'. It makes our lovely fresh air smell all nasty and makes far more noise than the motor boats. It has frightened away all the little birds. If I pray hard enough, it might just fall into the empty lock . . . not the people . . . just the car! It frightens me much more than the spiders or Isobel. I am sorry that this is such a long prayer. But I won't trouble you again for a long time. Thank you, God. Amen, straw . . . Sorry, I forgot."

New faces would appear at the weekends and some of the fishermen's wives would bring me copies of their weekly *Filmgoer* magazines. I cut out pictures of Jean Harlow, W C Fields, Our Gracie, Paul Robeson, Rudolph Valentino and many others and pasted them in a scrapbook.

At the end of the Reservoir bank, overlooking the Dingle, was a large wooden hut, used by the fishermen as a shelter. Father said it was well constructed and as solid as a rock. One night, a terrific gale blew up: it was March coming in like a lion. Father had been down the canal as far as the Halfway House, carrying out a late night lock inspection. He battled his way against the wind as he came back up the canal when he noticed a large black object floating towards the Dingle.

"Whatever that is," he said to himself, "without a pair of wings, I'll never catch up with it". He walked into the house and announced:

"Bugger me. I've just seen some huge thing flying off the Reservoir bank."

"Hmm," said Isobel with more than a hint of sarcasm, "Tommy Thompson's ale must have been a drop of the best tonight."

Father usually ignored Isobel's remarks because of the arguments that followed.

The next morning, he set out very early to inspect the storm damage. One big tree was uprooted, the punt had been blown right across the Reservoir and the fishermen's hut was nowhere to be seen.

"So I *did* see something flying through the air," thought Father. "I wasn't as sozzled as Isobel thought!"

After a good search, he found the shattered remains of the building among the trees in the Dingle.

The Dingle was among my favourite hidey-holes: a pretty spot right at the foot of the Reservoir bank. In Summer, the ground was covered by enormous ferns and they soon dried into masses of golden brown bracken. I would collect all the old household containers for my 'shop'. I made lovely mud pies sprinkled with sawdust and smashed apples in a bucket of water made a good cider brew (better, I thought, than Father's homemade 'poison'). I tied a rope from the lock gate to the garden fence to practice the high jump and I played hopscotch and bat and ball. Rarely was I bored. We had a long, wild orchard-cum-garden where I spent a long time looking under the gooseberry bush to see if I could find another 'me'! But (to my Father's delight) I was the only one that actually came 'from under the gooseberry bush'. I enjoyed eating the raw stalk of the cabbages, which I called the 'core'.

On long hot Summer evenings, Father and I would walk along the Reservoir banks looking for glow-worms, tiny moth-like creatures that could be discovered at twilight.

Tardebigge Reservoir is noted for the variety of wild flowers and I was never short of a posy to take home. Father taught me the names of every one: Meadow Sweet, Yarrow, Periwinkle, Foxglove, Ragged Robin, Lady's Smock, Cuckoo Pint, Mountain Everlasting, Catmint, Dead Nettle, Forget-me-not, Daisy, Elder, Mouse Ear, Red Campion, Saxifrage, Wild Strawberry, Traveller's Joy, Harebell, Bluebell, Coltsfoot, St John's Wort, Celandine, Honeysuckle, Stinking Hellebore, Convolvulus, Sneezewort, Gipsywort, Cowslip, Primrose, Dog Rose, Poppy, Comfrey, Bird's-foot Trefoil, Cuckoo Flower, Bedstraw, Shepherd's Purse, Deadly Nightshade, Vetch and Scarlet Pimpernel (the poorman's weather cock). There were many others, including numerous different kinds of thistle. Plenty were used for wines and herbal recipes.

At the back of the Reservoir were some very beautiful 'Whispering Aspen' trees: even when there was not a breath of wind or ripple on the water, the leaves would quiver ceaselessly. The Welsh call them *coed tafod merched*, 'the tree of the woman's tongue'!

After a day out hedge or wood cutting, it was always a great treat to start a bonfire to warm your hands and make your cheeks glow. As soon as the fire was really throwing out some heat, Father would bring some bread and a few slices of home-cured bacon. He would then strip the bark from a willow stick and thread the bacon on it. Soon the mouth-watering smell of 'sizzled' bacon came from the fire and I would be given one of the tastiest sandwiches I have ever eaten.

The Canada Geese arrived each year to make their nests and raise their young. There were also swans, moorhens, grebe, mallards, kingfishers, jays, woodpeckers and herons. Early one Spring morning there was great excitement as a small flight of birds gracefully skimmed the smooth surface of the Reservoir and decided to settle for a short time. We stood by the iron railings at the back of the house and watched as they rose, circled and landed once more. Shortly afterwards, they took off once more and climbed higher and higher in perfect formation. Later, we discovered they had been Arctic Terns. We never saw any again.

An exciting episode would be the arrival of Mr and Mrs Holmes and their Scout troop. They stayed fourteen long and glorious days and came laden with tents, billy cans, water buckets, and all the other paraphernalia necessary for their holiday. The most important item of equipment seemed to be the flag.

Once they had unpacked and the tents were pitched, we would all go off into the Dingle with hessian sacks which were filled with armfuls of bracken to make palliasses for the sleeping quarters. Each night, as soon as it was dusk, we sat in a circle around a campfire, drinking mugs of cocoa and singing songs like *The Quartermaster's Stores, Call John the Boatman* and *Campfires Burning*. This was almost the only time of the year I was allowed to stay up late. But at least it did give my Sister a chance to listen to the wireless. I would hope that Father would be late home from his singsong at the Halfway, and that I could stay a little longer.

In the Spring of 1930, one of the fishermen very kindly gave us a Marconi wireless. It was a portable set, powered by an accumulator of which we had two: one to use and one to take to

Cadbury campers enjoying a holiday by the Reservoir.

the shop and have charged. Woe betide us if the accumulator was flat for the Grand National or the Cup Final! Father delighted in actually hearing these live broadcasts instead of just reading about them. While the programmes were being relayed, I was not allowed to breathe, let alone speak.

The Cup Final was quite moving, with the huge crowd all singing *Abide with Me*, all as drunk as bob-howlers and as merry as crickets. On May 5 1930, we listened to the commentators' excited account of Amy Johnson's epic flight: 12,000 miles solo to Australia in a 24ft Gipsy Moth. She took a mere 19½ days, landed at Port Darwin on May 24 and arrived back home in England on August 6.

Tuesday teatime at 5.30pm, I listened to a lovely programme called Out with Romany by Bramwell Evans in the countryside with his Cocker Spaniel. It started in 1933 and lasted for many years. This was the only evening that I rushed home from school, because on Tuesdays I had to fetch the milk and cheese from Patchett's Farm and I didn't want to miss the programme. When it was over, I would hide in the 'privvy'. This was not to last long, for Sister's voice would come drifting up the garden path:

"I know you're in there! You get your backside off that closet seat, sitting there like Lady Godiva. Go and fetch the milk, and don't argue."

I wasn't going to argue. Wouldn't dream of it! It was quite a long walk to the farm – almost two miles. I could easily add another mile by the time the gander had chased me round the farmyard and over the fields. I arrived home hot, weary and very dusty. If there had been butter to collect it would all have turned to oil. And the milk . . .

"Where's all the milk gone, then, our Pat?" asked Sister, sourly. "Don't tell me you've upset it. There isn't a quart of milk in this can. And what about the cheese? I suppose the mice have been at it again."

There was something most tempting about fresh farm cheese!

During the hot Summer days, when the air felt like a damp, warm blanket, it was essential to scald the milk to prevent it going sour. This was a drawnout process involving bringing it up to boiling point in a porringer or double saucepan over a low burner on the oil stove. To prevent the water boiling dry, the pan was stood on an asbestos mat.

When I was a child, Patchett's Farm was run by the Frazier brothers. Before the Great War, they had owned a narrow boat called *John Bull*. It was used to transport their annual coal supply to take produce into Birmingham and to return with horse manure for the crops.

The Summer of 1929 brought a heatwave, followed by a severe drought. Father prophesied that 'tempest was brewing', meaning that a violent thunderstorm would break the unbearable, stifling weather. Sister rushed around the house, covering the mirrors with sheets and hiding away in drawers anything like cutlery that might act as a lightening conductor.

The reservoir was almost empty. I was playing on a patch of ground called 'The Island'. Most of the Reservoir wells were now visible and the deepest one was on this ground, fenced off for safety. Thin trickles of water connected a few small puddles. The clay bed was dry and cracked. Even the little Marsh Cinquefoil hung its pretty little head in the hope of rain. Tony was having a wonderful time, digging in the clay with his front paws in the search for buried treasure: a dead fish or perhaps the remains of a small bird.

Maybe the storm would blow over, then I could stay here much longer. Anyhow, I wasn't afraid of tempest and lightening and once the storm was over, we would have the most beautiful rainbow. I thought:

"I'll sit here and keep very quiet and recite the very first poem I learned." It was called *The Rainbow:*

> "Two little clouds one summer day
> Went rolling through the sky.
> They went so fast, they bumped their heads
> And both began to cry.
> Old Father Sun looked out and said
> Oh, never mind my dears.
> I'll send my little fairy folk
> To dry your falling tears.
> One fairy came in violet and one in indigo;
> In blue, red, yellow, orange and green,
> They made a pretty row."

"Now that I've recited my poem to Tony, he isn't frightened either!"

It must have been almost teatime, because I was feeling hungry. It was also getting dark. Father was calling very anxiously and there was a distant rumble (not my tummy, I thought). I rushed over to the house, followed by Tony, as fast as my little legs would go. Just as we got inside, a flash of lightening shot through the sky, followed by a quite deafening clap of thunder. Poor Tony dashed into the corner and wriggled behind the treadle of the sewing machine, his favourite place if a storm was brewing.

Suddenly, the whole world went black. Even the leather on the chair was hot and sticky and it was almost impossible to sit down. Was this the end of the world that I had heard the grown-ups talking about? By now, it was virtually impossible to see across the living room. Every door and window was propped open and a heavy grey mist filled the house, making it difficult to breathe properly. This was a totally new experience for me. It was very eerie.

The thunder and lightening was now continuous. I was sitting on Father's lap, feeling very sleepy, wondering how much longer the storm could last. Then, there was a terrific bang: the lightening had struck the electric poles in the garden and smashed the crock insulators. This was followed by a loud 'ping' from the telephone bell and a small ball of light appeared to leave the 'phone, float around the room and drift out through the open door. Little did I realise then what a fortunate person I was to witness this spectacle. Never since have I seen or heard of this happening.

After a heavy storm, it was not unusual to be inundated with a plague of tiny black midges. They swarmed into the house in a black cloud, soon covering the windows like a black net curtain. The only way to be rid of them was to spray the windows with soapsuds. Even then, it was impossible to remove them in one operation.

During the Summer of 1933, an extensive repair job was carried out by the lock keepers, dredger's gang and other maintenance staff. It had been noticed that the Reservoir was losing large quantities of water daily. The heavy gear was brought down the canal by boat and it was no easy task moving it across to the Reservoir. A large platform was constructed in the deepest water, its legs sunk deep in the mud. It was about a week before the structure was level and safe for the men to work on.

The following week, a diver arrived with all his equipment: diving suit, helmet, boots and pump. All this was most exciting. I was rushing up and down the Reservoir bank with jugs of tea and bottles of homemade pop.

"Don't thee fergit to bring a swig of thee ferther's homemade wallop!"

After the men had 'wet their whistles', I saw the diver dress up for his descent into the deep, murky water. His job was to inspect the pipe and repair the valve which released water out of the Reservoir, into the culvert, down through the Dingle and back into the canal during the course of water-running.

The diver was a young man in his early thirties. Once inside his waterproof suit, two of the men helped him on with the helmet. This was like a big metal bowl, strong and quite heavy. A glass window was fitted into the front while his airpipe connected at the back. The helmet locked onto a metal neckband and was secured in place by wingnuts. A lifeline was then attached round his waist and all was ready for his adventure into the unknown. As he started down the ladder into the water, two of the men began to turn a wheel to pump air into the helmet.

The going was hard and the equipment heavy. There was no underwater lighting, so all repairs were carried out by touch. He was able to stay down for only a short time. Upon this simple equipment there hung a man's life! I found it thrilling!

The diver and his support team. Father in the white hat.

CHAPTER TEN

Epilogue

MANY years ago, Father had told me that in the dim and distant future the Engine House would be sold and turned into a road house. A place for dancing and entertainment.

"You mark my words, my lass, I know that I shall never live to see it, but in years to come you'll remember what I've told you. You'll see. One day."

It was an ideal spot, he said, with access from the Old London Road for all the cars. And anyone that had had a skinful, well, you could chuck them in the cut to cool off. If you didn't like the company you were with, you could take them out and chuck them in as well!

So, after standing cold and empty for many years, in 1975, the Engine House received a new face. Planning consent was obtained for a conversion to a restaurant and country club. Most of the old building was preserved. The original brick floor was polished, bright little lights glimmered in the canal and the sound of music was carried along on the breeze.

The Worcester & Birmingham Canal carried freight traffic for about 145 years. It had changed surprisingly little since the days when it was dug out by gangs of navvies. The water was never very clean, but it was constantly flowing. Nationalisation came in 1948 and it was transferred to the British Waterways Board in 1962. Many of the lock keepers' cottages are now private houses, all modernised. When a friend who works for the Midlands Electricity Board said that he had been to read the meter in my old house, it only dawned on me later what changes must have taken place.

The Halfway House, scene of many bygone happy hours, was sold in 1963 and continued as licensed premises for a number of years. It is now a private residence, but there must remain many silent shadows from the past. Patchett's Farm is unchanged except that the little path – 'my' little path- from the bottom of the Reservoir bank to the farm, is now lost in a ploughed field. Along it, I knew every stone and every tree, every bush and every berry.

Each night, my little legs carried me back and forth as I swung the milk can and sang loud enough to drown the noise of the threshing machine in the next field. This was my 'milky way': my escape from the washing up!

Hill Cottage, a landmark a few hundred yards away from the foot of the Reservoir bank, has now been demolished, but the little house at the top of Grimley Lane remains occupied.

A main arterial road, the A38 Bromsgrove Highway now runs parallel with the church and school. The old road is still there, winding past the Village Hall and the Hewell Lodges, down over Tardebigge Tunnel, through Tutnall and Finstall and into Aston Fields. No longer can you quietly wander from the church down the little School Lane to the Lodge at the entrance to Hewell park. The Village Hall was bought by a brewery in 1945 when the Hewell Estate was broken up. To begin with it was The Tardebigge licensed restaurant and bar; then for a while it stood empty and isolated, alone with its memories of music and laughter and children's voices; the applause of the Christmas pantos; the crack of bowls as they rolled down the green and shouts from the cricket teams on a warm Summer's evening.

In the Winter of 1981, I set out with a friend to meet the Area Manager from Ansell's Brewery, in order to take photographs of the fine bas reliefs inside. The building was cold and dark and I had no wish to stay longer than was necessary. Subsequently, the Village Hall changed hands again and was extensively altered. Very sadly, the bas reliefs with their associations with Clive of India and the Plymouth family, were broken up and cast onto a heap of rubble.

Hewell Grange is a Government Borstal Training Establishment, but is little changed outside. Open days are rare, and somehow I had always seemed to miss them. I was longing to see the place again, having heard many conflicting reports. At last, after nearly fifty years, I was able to retrace my steps and to walk along the familiar corridors once more. The Deputy Governor and several members of staff treated me like a VIP. I asked if I might walk from the courtyard and down the passage which leads to the Ballroom. The corridor is now lined with small offices, but even these could not prevent the happy memories from flooding back, just as though it had all happened yesterday. Children in their party clothes, walking in pairs, holding hands. Chattering, happy little people, without a care in the world. One thing that was missing was my little naked cherub! I walked again over the still polished floor of the Great Hall. I could almost hear the sound of crackers banging and see the much coveted doll's house which had stood near the entrance to the main staircase.

The church is just the same as always. So is the frontage of the schoolhouse. A small extension has been grafted onto the side of the school and the old barn has weathered over the years.

Plymouth Guest House is now a private nursing home. Each time I hear the name mentioned, I recall a little girl in a red velvet dress walking past on a Sunday morning to collect the paper from the blacksmith's house on the Wharf. Heaven alone knows where the money came from to buy the material for that dress.

The Reservoir continues to be fished by members of the Bournville Angling Club. But what has happened to the air of excitement that used to make the place so alive? Where did it all vanish to? Maybe it was the War that changed our ways. Many of the young men for whom I carried jugs of tea went off to fight and never returned. The older ones are now all dead.

Where did all the narrow boats go and what happened to all those busy little places that once thrived and bubbled over with life? The answer to all this can be summed up in a single word . . .

One of the series of bas reliefs depicting events in the Plymouth family history and placed in the Village Hall as a memorial to the 1st Earl (1857–1923).

Progress. But are we really any better for it?

Who can tell? One day we may even see the return of the horsedrawn canal boat.

Opposite, is the very last photograph of Father, John Warner. Lock keeper and Water Bailiff, Worcester & Birmingham Canal. It was taken at the end of a career that had spanned sixty years. Born October 20 1880. Died May 24 1952.

This time, instead of me outside the house, Father holds the hand of his grandson Peter, my son. Right up to the end he wore his old leather belt with his windlass tucked in it. He never had a holiday; never spent a day at the seaside. He made himself content with whatever the Lord chose to send to him. Perhaps his secret hope was that, one day, his 'ship might come home.' That was not to be. He always said:

"What I have never had, I've never missed."

In the Spring of 1952, it became obvious that years of hard work and sweated labour had begun to take their toll. No longer did Father take a stroll down the Reservoir bank. He began to lose interest in the sights and sounds which had been his lifelong pleasures. He could remember walking the towpath as a very small child, holding his father's hand. As I had held his and my son Peter, after me.

I soon realised that the end of an era was in sight. There would be no more walks along the cut side, no more songs at the Halfway. This would be the end of jugs of tea and fishing tickets.

What would become of Isobel? How would she settle to a different way of life? She was getting older now, and I knew in my heart that she would never be happy elsewhere. If she left, as leave she would have to, she would always long to return. But return to what? Certainly not to the old life which she had come to accept.

As for me, I had left home at the age of seventeen to become a student nurse. These were the War years and life had suddenly become unsettled for everyone.

After Father died, Isobel was obliged to look for another home. Unable to stay in Tardebigge, she took a post as a cook in a hospital at Erdington, on the other side of Birmingham. Within six months, she contracted a terminal illness which lasted for twelve long years. It was I who travelled back and forth to Birmingham, shopped and washed and cooked for her and made numerous visits to her in hospital. All this was fitted in between my full-time District Nursing and raising my family. Eventually, she was so ill

Father with his one and only Grandchild – Peter, 1950.

that it was necessary for her to come and live with us.

The only thing she asked of life was to reach her sixtieth year and then she could retire. The day before that birthday, she realised that I had been put on earth for a purpose and that fate had been kind to her, after all. Isobel reached her sixtieth birthday on Boxing Day, 1964.

She died the following day.

My feelings about Tardebigge are very mixed. Sometimes happy, sometimes sad. Although I lived quite nearby, I had not returned in almost thirty years. Then, one Sunday in the Spring of 1981, I retraced my steps and relived many many memories as I drove from the Engine House, down the Dust House Lane, up Grimley Lane and along to what is now the Bournville Angling Club Car Park.

I scrambled up the Reservoir bank which was wet and slippery, hanging onto every blade of grass I could grab. A lot of water had run under the bridge since I last attempted this and I was a bit out of puff by the time I had reached the top.

I stood for a moment and gazed across the cold, grey, uninviting water. A large notice warned: "These waters are deep and dangerous." There were a number of people about and I thought that I must be the only one there who really knew just how deep they were. Here, I used to play on the edge of these waters. I would take the punt out and row across to the other side. I never saw any dangers. Just as well there wasn't any notice to warn me!

As I stood there dreaming, it occurred to me that I wouldn't allow my grandchildren to play here. It was quite alarming.

I didn't go to the house. I wanted to remember it as it had been. For a minute, I listened to the waves lapping at the bank and I was sure I could hear that lovely old song again, drifting over the water: *The Old House* by Sir Frederick O'Connor:

"Gone are the old folk,
No light in the window.
No more to their homes shall these children return.
Why stand I here like a ghost, like a shadow?
It's time I was going.
It's time I passed on."

Lamplight no long shines through the window. Electricity has taken its place. The canal water looked still and stagnant; unused and unloved.

Four generations at Lock 53. Top left: *Mother, A. J. Turner and Father.* Top right: *Pat, the Nurse, 1929.* Bottom left: *my son Peter, with Betty Tilt from Patchett's Farm, 1951.* Bottom right: *Peter's son Brent, 1981.*

So many dreams, so many voices come drifting slowly back, echoes of bygone days.

Tommy Thompson, calling the cattle.

The Fraziers at Patchett's Farm, shouting at the gander.

The boat children calling out: "Got any apples, Mr Warner?"

And a fisherman's voice coming across the water on a still night: "I've got a bite and it's a big one!"

And always Father's voice singing "My world for ever, the sunshine of your smile."

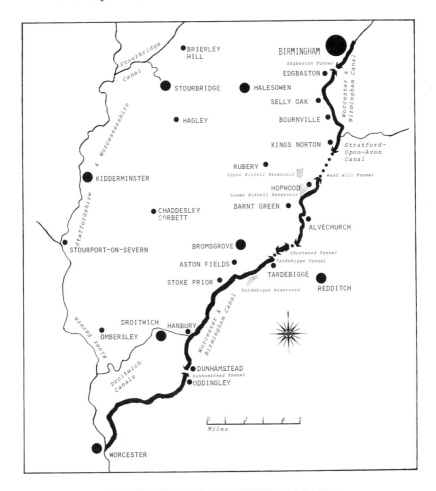

THE WORCESTER & BIRMINGHAM CANAL
Gas Street Basin, Birmingham to the River Severn at Diglis Basin, Worcester. Opened to traffic in 1815. 30 miles in length, with 58 locks.

*Meeting with Harold Jones from Cadbury, my old childhood fishing
friend, 1987.*